Mrs Moneypenny: Survival in the City

Mrs Moneypenny: Survival in the City

PIATKUS

Visit the Piatkus website!

Piatkus publishes a wide range of best-selling fiction and non-fiction, including books on health, mind, body & spirit, sex, self-help, cookery, biography and the paranormal.

If you want to:
- read descriptions of our popular titles
- buy our books over the internet
- take advantage of our special offers
- enter our monthly competition
- learn more about your favourite Piatkus authors

VISIT OUR WEBSITE AT: www.piatkus.co.uk

First published in 2003 by
Judy Piatkus (Publishers) Limited
5 Windmill Street
London WIT 2JA
e-mail: info@piatkus.co.uk

The moral right of the author has been asserted

A catalogue record for this book is available from the British Library

ISBN 0 7499 2416 0

Edited by Ian Paten
Text design by Paul Saunders
Alex cartoons by Charles Peattie

This book has been printed on paper manufactured
with respect for the environment using wood from
managed sustainable resources

Typeset by Phoenix Photosetting, Chatham, Kent
Printed and bound in Great Britain by
Mackays Ltd, Chatham

Dedication

*This book is dedicated to Mr M and to sons number one,
two and three, who put up with me for the years that
I worked in the City*

Contents

Acknowledgements

Writing a book when you have a full-time job, several regular newspaper and magazine columns, and are finishing a PhD thesis at the same time, is complete madness. It would also have been completely impossible if it were not for several people who have acted as midwife and inspiration. My thanks go to, in no particular order, Judy Piatkus for having the idea, my editors Gill Bailey and Anna Crago for coaxing it out of me, my agent Peter Robinson for helping me navigate the paperwork and everyone with whom I have ever worked or been associated with in the City who has supplied the anecdotes within. My Girlfriends have been key to my welfare and survival during the process, and my thanks go to them also. Finally, to all the readers of my column, both in the *Financial Times* and the *Financial News*, who have written to me over the years – you are the people who have made me think this was a project worth doing. Thank you!

Mrs Moneypenny
April 2003

Introduction

THIS BOOK HAS BEEN WRITTEN by a middle-aged mother of three who spent almost all of her thirties working in an investment bank. It presents my view of what it was like to work in investment banking in the 1990s – not ignoring the gargantuan bonuses, the excessive expense claims and the groundless arrogance that characterised the City for most of that decade. It is also an insight into the City now.

Why should you be reading it? Even if you do not work in the City, the chances are that you personally contribute to how the City functions. If, for instance, you bought this book in a shop owned by a publicly quoted company, then you have directly contributed to its income and your few pounds will appear, added to many more, in its financial results, which will be scrutinised by many highly paid people in the Square Mile. Even if you borrowed it or acquired it in a jumble sale, more than likely you have a bank account, you save money, you borrowed to buy your home. All of these activities, singly or together, mean that you participate, if somewhat vicariously, in the activities of the City.

I entered the City at the age of 30 with a newly minted MBA from the London Business School and got out just before my 39th birthday. The month after I left, equity volumes halved and everything started to go horribly wrong. You may think this was an extraordinarily well-planned move, but of course it was simply an accident of timing. During my tenure I managed to organise postings to Hong Kong, Singapore and Japan, and along the way I encountered egos the size of mountains, working practices and environments that would test anyone and hedonism on a scale that you can only imagine. I also learned the true art of sycophancy, so crucial in a client service industry. And I survived – just. But this isn't just my story. It's the story of a whole cast of characters and even a whole way of life.

What goes on in the City is not rocket science, even if people tell you it is. It is simply a large number of individuals and companies pushing money around from place to place and taking a bit out for themselves en route. Read on and discover what exactly they get up to, as well as how to survive there for as long as I did – or longer. But whether you work in the City yourself, or once did, or are the wife, husband, child, parent, friend, lover or mistress of someone who does, or aspire to work there, this book is relevant to you.

Why me? I had wanted to work in the City from a very young age. When I was 13 my economics teacher explained to my class the inverse relationship between the rate of interest and the price of bonds (in other words, when one goes down the other goes up) and I was hooked. From that day I was determined that eventually I would work in the City, that I too would help to move millions of pounds around from place to place. Apart from my gap-year job working in the back office of a government bond trading operation, I didn't make it into the City proper until I was 30, eight years after I graduated. I had worked in an advertising agency (a quoted company, having floated on the London Stock Exchange the previous year) and subsequently in financial PR, on several privatisations. Then I worked for another public company, in pharmaceuticals, taking care of all its communications with the professional investment community – the City. All this felt like a dress rehearsal for the real thing. I traded my honeymoon for a place on an MBA programme at the London Business School, determined to take up a position on a trading floor. When I finally made it, in every sense it lived up to expectations, but it also blew apart my theory that it was in any way an intellectually challenging pastime.

So I was not typical of today's graduate intake. I was already married, already had one child who was not yet three. Many of the people that I initially worked for were far younger than me. My observations of the City I joined were therefore those of a more mature person, someone who had a slightly different perspective to that of a raw graduate straight in from Oxbridge.

There are many people in the City who earned more money than I ever did. There are many who worked on bigger deals, filed bigger expense claims, hung out with bigger clients. But the view of the City from 30,000 feet is not the only view. I spent more than eight years in the thick of the financial markets, observing the chaos at first hand. In many ways I was the most unexceptional of City employees, in other ways unique. In less than nine years I held nine different jobs in four different countries on two different continents. I proved that adaptability, practicality and, above all, resilience were required to survive. The City isn't a man's world – it's a shark's world. Just like a shark you have to keep moving to survive. Stand still for a minute and it's all over.

* * *

Over the years I worked for several different men. Most of them were delightful, and some of them were complete shits. For some reason I never worked for a woman, unless you count a brief stint right at the end when I was allocated the task of propping up a chain-smoking executive with an apparent eating disorder and an ability to thrive on nervous energy. One of my favourite bosses was my Far Too Nice Boss. He had enjoyed a stellar career in the City before encountering me, and I knew from the first time I set eyes on him that we were in for an interesting time. FTNB is now one of those charming men in their forties who has a twinkle in the eye and makes the most of his ability to listen intently and focus on people as if they were the only thing in his universe that mattered.

FTNB didn't want a stellar career in the City. His father had had one, which is enough to put anyone off. Most children of City stars want to work elsewhere. At university he found his real love, which was broadcasting. In the late 1970s he was an integral part of the university radio station, commandeering the airwaves every morning with his breakfast show. Highly focused in his ambitions, he knew exactly where he wanted his career to start after graduation – at the BBC.

Sadly for him the BBC did not share his enthusiasm. Thwarted by their selection procedure, he had to settle for a job at Cazenove instead – presumably very much second best in his eyes. Cazenove is a company that could arguably be said to be the last bastion of gentlemanly capitalism. It was – and is – full of very pleasant people. It is not surprising that, having started life in the City there, FTNB learned to be Far Too Nice. He hates to offend. This, of course, means that sometimes he ends up offending even more people. Women adore him, and men find him a sympathetic listener and a wise observer on the financial markets. He came to have quite an impact on my career, as you will see.

*   *   *

When, after seven years in the City, my telephone rang in Tokyo in June 1999, I was exceptionally busy, effectively running the Japanese branch of an investment bank, with 220 people to manage, plus a home comprising three children (one not even six months old) and a husband, at the same time as studying for my PhD. My lady caller couldn't have been more charming. Would I consider writing a weekly column for a new magazine being launched to accompany the weekend *Financial Times*? My reply was unprintable – where did she think I was going to find the time? But she persevered, and so I ended up sharing my family and professional life every week for almost four years with readers in the weekend *FT*, and more recently in the *Financial News*.

That's why me, in a nutshell. I have written this book for anyone with an interest in the City, from aspiring undergraduates who have heard that the streets of London are paved with gold (or at least sign-on bonuses that will help to pay off their student loans) to octogenarians whose grandchildren are 'something in the City'. If you already work there, it is also for you, because I have views on everything in the

Introduction

Square Mile, from equal pay for women (it has always been equal, in my opinion) to the pricing structure of lap-dancing establishments (an open-and-shut case for referral to the Competition Commission, if you ask me). In between I look at such key topics as the IQ of equity salesmen, the independence of investment research and the complete nonsense that is the guaranteed bonus. So even if I have to explain a few things that you already understand, you may enjoy seeing whether or not you agree with my opinions. And you may even find that you appear in one of the many anecdotes, apocryphal or otherwise, that crop up throughout the book.

This is not a textbook. It will not help you get through any examination. It is a very personal book, a view of the City from the highly subjective viewpoint of one woman, a working mother who spent nearly nine years as a wage slave to the shareholders of a large bank.

I enjoyed almost every moment of my time in the City. I hope that you enjoy this book even half as much.

Getting Started in the City

Getting Started in the City

THE VERY TITLE OF THIS BOOK, *Survival in the City,* implies that the City is somewhere where survival is not a foregone conclusion. But where is this place, 'the City', and why does it need surviving within?

The City of London is both the name of a geographical place (the area comprising London postcodes EC1, 2, 3 and 4) and the term used to refer to the financial services industry that originated in the area. The two are no longer synonymous, although much of what goes on in the physical place is connected with the industry.

What is this industry that keeps so many people employed at such inflated salaries? It is the business of financial intermediation. A financial intermediary is someone who interposes themselves between savers and borrowers of money. There are so many ways to save (and invest) money, and so many ways to borrow (and acquire) it, that the chances of two people with matching profiles meeting up and agreeing to exchange their money are almost nil.

Thus the men and women of 'the City' act as the people in the middle.

I am writing this book in the middle of the longest downturn in the stock market since the Second World War. Is the City finished, therefore? The answer is, and will always be, no, for two reasons. Companies that make and sell things will always need money to grow, to fund working capital, to build new factories and processing plants. Even service companies need money to develop and grow. That money comes via the City (the industry as opposed to the place, although it may be both). Equally, individuals such as you and me are continuing to set aside money for our pensions, especially as the government increasingly urges us to do so. So money continues to be saved, and continues to be needed.

Whether a company needing money borrows it as a loan from one of a number of banks, or issues bonds (literally IOUs) or shares (tiny proportions of the company that people can own), it will have to use third parties to handle the process. These third parties are not the users of money; they are the fixers and dealers, who work for the greater glory of capitalism. They are the people who work in the City.

* * *

As Dan Atkinson said in *The Complete Guide to the Financial Markets*, 'moving money is not an overly glamorous task, and its importance to the national economy, while considerable, is far from critical'. So why would anyone want to work in the City? The financial attractions are no doubt very appealing. Graduates starting in September 2003 can expect to earn initial salaries of £40,000 and qualify for sign-on bonuses of a few thousand pounds to assist with paying off their student loans. At the other end of the scale it is possible to earn millions in salary and bonuses without having to go through the usual wealth-creating avenue of setting up a business.

It never fails to amaze me that young people leaving university are so desperate to work 'in the City'. You have to understand that when I graduated (from Newcastle University) in 1984, the City was not an obvious destination for a female graduate, albeit one with a quasi-economics degree. Rightly or wrongly, in the early 1980s the City was still seen as the preserve of ex-army officers and the like. Graduates with good degrees went into the civil service or the BBC or even – can you believe it? – advertising agencies. The City was simply not regarded as a career option by the vast majority of able and accomplished graduates. Many young people of my generation could not see the attraction of going to work somewhere where one simply 'moved money around'.

It is always interesting to read how other people got started in the City. Two of the best published accounts I have read are those of Michael Lewis in *Liar's Poker* and Philip Augar in *The Death of Gentlemanly Capitalism*. Lewis tells of how he sat next to the wife of a prominent investment banker at Salomon Brothers at a charity event. She appeared to decide on a whim that he should be working in investment banking and propelled him into employment courtesy of her husband. Reading this, people outside the City will no doubt regard this as a prime example of cronyism, but in practice this is of course how many people get their jobs – not only in the City but elsewhere.

After writing off to several merchant banks, Augar was offered two interviews. The first was scheduled for 2.30 p.m., and he describes arriving and then waiting on a comfortable sofa, reading glossy magazines about the countryside.

> Just before 3.00, a chap ambled in, clearly having enjoyed a good lunch, and asked me a few introductory questions: school (grammar), university (Cambridge), contacts in the City (none), sports played (lots). I was on the alert: this was just to wrong-foot me and there would be a tough question on the economy any minute. But no, the next comment was, "Well you seem like a decent type, we'll offer you a job". The time was 3.20 p.m.; I had been with him less than half an hour, and I left elated at my performance, one that had been so brilliant that I had landed a job within minutes.

This filled him with as much horror as it does us:

> On the train on the way home doubts set in: he seemed drunk; would he remember the offer in the morning? Even if he did remember, did I really want to work for people who took decisions on the hoof, were late for meetings, drank heavily at lunch, kept no records, and thought their guests would enjoy reading about hunting, fishing and shooting?

Augar goes on to describe the other interview, conducted over lunch, which resulted in an offer that he accepted.

* * *

When I left the London Business School in 1992 with an MBA, deeply indebted to a high-street bank, I knew what I wanted to do – I wanted to be a general equities salesman. For those of you unfamiliar with this particular vocation, let me explain. Armies of people sit at computer screens on trading floors, and their job is to communicate their employer's views of the stock market events of the day to their fund management clients. This can involve wide-ranging discussions, and involves spending a lot of time on the telephone or meeting these clients, building a relationship with them and working out which news and research they are most likely to need so that you can provide an exemplary service. To me, this seemed like the ideal job.

It always helps to know exactly what you want to do when you are looking for a position in the City, and why it is that you think you would be exceptionally suited to that task. Although most training schemes allow for rotation around the organisation, which in theory allows a good inside look before making a decision, this doesn't always work out because of the massive amount of infighting in every bank over who pays for graduate training schemes. If corporate finance, for example, are paying to support five people through the graduate training scheme then they want to know that those five people are headed for corporate finance afterwards.

One of the problems facing young people seeking to enter the City today is that they have no real conception of what people actually do there. The process of graduate admissions is quite extraordinary, and completely different to my own experience. Most banks undertake a process similar to the following. A number of senior executives go round the country in the autumn term, only bothering with the top six universities, giving open presentations with free alcohol and whipping the student population into a frenzy about how exciting and dynamic the City is as a place to work. (In my last years in the Square Mile I was closely involved with recruitment and was regularly put on the podium.) After this grand presentation tour, some 3,000 or so undergraduates apply to each investment bank. In our case these were then reduced to about 250 using the most arbitrary criteria. Had they got a maths A-level? What was their predicted university grade? Once the pile had been whittled down to 250 everyone was seen for a first interview by the personnel department, and only about 100 would actually be put in front of any practitioners. At the end of the process, including jobs in IT and in the back office (where the paperwork is processed), it is likely that no more than forty or so people would be offered a job – and sometimes fewer.

My own case was different. I was older, and had had the privilege of working on the fringes of the City for some considerable time beforehand. I had effectively been putting the investment case for one business for five years and was desperate to have more variety in my life. I knew I could sell, I knew I understood what makes companies tick, and I enjoyed talking to fund managers – the people who actually make the decisions to buy or sell stocks and shares. All of these things in my opinion made me an excellent candidate for a UK generalist equity salesperson. I could think of nothing more interesting at the time than arriving at my desk every day, being able to talk on the telephone about a wide-ranging number of stocks to an eclectic but fascinating group of fund managers. I would be able to read and research information on anything up to 3,000 companies. There were then some 2,000 companies quoted on the London Stock Exchange, and any stockbroker worth its salt would cover at least the top 200, and then there would probably be another couple of hundred in which it had a special interest. I would at last be liberated from telling the same story over and over again, and would be in a position where I would have up to 400 different stories to sell every day. I seriously couldn't think of anything more exciting.

I carefully researched how I was going to get this idyllic job, and who I was going to target. I rang up the four companies that a friendly fund manager had suggested were seeking to expand their sales staff, and established who was head of UK equity sales in each. I then crafted a carefully composed letter to each of the four, attaching my CV and explaining my familiarity with UK fund managers. I was interviewed by all four, and offered a job by two. It sounds easy; in fact it was anything but.

I won't bother mentioning the interviews I had with the three companies I did not join. By contrast, my series of interviews with the company I *did* join are well worth describing. The initial interview was, as expected, with the head of UK equity sales to whom I had written. He was clearly reasonably impressed with my enthusiasm and understanding of the markets and agreed with my conviction that I could sell. My second interview was with a senior salesman – or rather, saleswoman, a very capable one, which reinforced my conviction that this was somewhere I wanted to work. She thought that perhaps general equities wasn't the best area for my skills, and suggested that I might make an excellent specialist salesperson and support to a team of analysts.

A specialist salesperson sells more than one stock but in very few (usually one or two) sectors – say pharmaceuticals, or engineering. They are also called marketing analysts, or even talking analysts. Their job is to work closely with a team of people who are analysing and valuing companies in a particular sector and then convey their thoughts to the outside world. At the end of the day their prime job is to make the lead analyst in the team famous. Provided this chap (or woman, but it is more usually a man) is right up there in the client's estimation, they are doing well. It is not a job that anybody does for personal glory, but the more famous you can make your team the better rewarded you will be.

It wasn't exactly what I was looking for – I could see the number of stocks that I would be able to learn about shrinking from 400 to nearer 20 – but it was a job, nonetheless. I was then interviewed by the team – or rather by the two most senior analysts in it. Two more arrogant people I had yet to meet, and I can't say that it was a particularly comfortable hour. If these were the chaps I was going to have to put on the map, I didn't think much of my chances. In any event, I decided that if this was the way in I was going to knuckle down and accept it. They, however, were not so convinced. Indeed, they offered the job to someone else, a girl already working in specialist sales in another investment bank.

I was depressed about this, but my earlier interviewer, a bright and capable woman, as I said, had now got the bit between her teeth and was determined I should not escape the net. I was thus proposed as a salesperson to the smaller-companies team and interviewed by a senior member of that team. This was possibly the most disastrous interview that anybody could ever have had. He was a bachelor who had spent many years not seeing the need for women in or around his home or workplace, and I can't imagine what he thought of me. He spent most of the first part of the interview telling me how little money I would earn, and how by starting in the City at the advanced age of 30 I would effectively be going back to the drawing board and clawing my way up from scratch. I told him I knew this, had thought about it very carefully, and was completely prepared for it; my application was hardly a random event. He then went on to say that he didn't really approve of hiring women, because they inevitably left the City after an expensive training to get married and have a family.

Ten years later, it seems incredible that I didn't walk out there and then and telephone a lawyer. At the time I was completely incensed, not least because I was of course already married with a two-year-old child. However, I don't wear a wedding ring and no family information appears on my CV. I swallowed hard and told my interviewer that this was not going to be an issue he would ever have with me, but stopped short of volunteering why. However, he was not pacified by this assurance. After the third time of being told that it was very unlikely that anybody was going to hire me, as I was bound to fall in love, get married and be whisked away from the trading floor to a life of domestic servitude, I decided I could bear it no longer and put him straight. I explained that this was very unlikely to happen to me as I had already walked down the aisle with somebody, and had already produced a child who was now safely ensconced in one of central London's private nursery schools.

(At this point I should explain why I don't wear a wedding ring. Six months after my marriage, and already three months pregnant with my first child, I was sitting in a meeting drafting documentation with a group of investment bankers. The meeting went on late into the evening, and eventually someone decided to order some food. Going round the table and taking pizza orders, they came to me and stopped. 'Oh, Mrs M, we forgot you were here. Are you all right to stay late? Will Mr M mind?'

I was appalled by this. Did they not credit me with enough intelligence to have already calculated how late I was going to be and make the necessary arrangements to forewarn my husband? Indeed, the implication that nobody else in the room needed to be consulted about their wife, but I needed to be consulted about my husband, was enough to get me to go home that night, take off my wedding ring and never put it back on again.)

My interviewer then berated me for not wearing a ring, demanded to know why this information was not on my CV, and asked me how much money my husband earned. I told him that I wasn't prepared to disclose this information. I was then told that I clearly would not be suitable – as the pampered wife of a well-paid man (I wish!), I would obviously regard this job as just a hobby. In the opinion of my interviewer, my husband was bound to be supporting me, making it unlikely that I would be entirely focused at work and prepared to give the commitment the company would require.

I had by this time realised that I was never, ever going to contemplate working in the same building as this man. However, I didn't get up and storm off like an insulted guest on a chat show. I very politely thanked my interviewer for his time, walked out of the room and left the building, assuming that I was never going to return.

After this Mr M and I took our two-year-old off to the West Country for a few days' R&R. Such a 'break' with a two-year-old is always enough to make me completely exhausted, and I kept my mobile phone on at all times to encourage interruptions. A charming young man, another equity salesperson working on the desk with my original female sponsor, called. He had heard of my somewhat combative interview from her and wondered whether I would be prepared to come back again.

I made the very valid point to him that this would be my fifth interview with no prospect of employment, and that I was sick of paying the train fare from Isleworth or taking taxis to EC2. He immediately offered to pay my travel expenses, humble though they were, which made a sufficiently good impression on me that I agreed to meet him. Face to face, he was quite unlike anyone I had encountered in the City thus far. Sensible and reasonable, even to the point of wearing (in high summer) a vest under his shirt, presumably to stop excessive perspiration from ruining the look, he was the bespectacled product of a redbrick university, and I was immediately charmed. Here at last was somebody who wasn't arrogant, wasn't pushy and had a few brain cells to rub together. He was very careful to apologise for the behaviour of my previous interviewer, and also explained that the first choice of the Arrogant Twosome for the position of specialist salesperson had declined to take up the offer as she had fallen pregnant (it can happen to anyone!) and so the position was now open once more. Would I be prepared to consider it?

After the misogynist smaller-companies man, I considered that the Arrogant Twosome were a piece of cake by comparison, and that at the very least I should be able to ingratiate myself with a reasonable amount of hard work. So it was that my entry to the City was indeed as a specialist salesperson, supporting a team led by two men of vastly different ages and intellects, both of whom were supremely convinced of their own capabilities.

* * *

I have done more than my fair share of giving people a start on the career ladder in the City. I don't have any compunction about this – while I can always help people in, whether or not they succeed will be completely up to them. I have no problem with nepotism as a means of opening the door; where things can go awry is if advancement is made on the basis of friendship rather than ability. However, that rarely happens in the City these days. Once you are in, it is strictly a meritocracy.

Not everybody that I have helped has succeeded, but I am pleased to say that many of them have. There is a particularly able transport analyst, now well established in his sector, who I fought tooth and nail to get a permanent job for after he had accomplished an especially good temporary assignment for me. From then on, in terms of both aptitude and loyalty, he has turned out to be a much better pick than the graduate intake that arrived at more or less the same time. And yet this is a guy who would never have even made it beyond the first round of any formulaic selection process. Although he had been to a top university, he didn't have a suitably quantitative degree or even the right A-levels. He is also softly spoken, and not aggressive at interviews. I am delighted that I saw something that perhaps would not have been apparent if he had come in through the normal routes, and I am terribly proud of him now.

Similarly, a few years ago a lingerie shop assistant I was talking to asked me what I did for a living. When, in between being fitted for a bra, I told her that I was involved in the stock market she explained that her daughter, a product of one of London's top private girls' schools and with an excellent degree from Oxford, as well as several European languages, was desperate to get into the City and had been turned down by every bank she had applied to. This sounded like an exceptional waste of talent to me, so I handed over my card and invited her to get her daughter to call me. This duly happened, and I am delighted to say that she too, after a bit of a pep talk from me and some guidance about how to apply, went back into the application process a second time and will be happily into her second year of employment by the time this book comes out.

The point of these examples is not to bang on about my benevolence. Everyone I know who works in the City has at some time or another given someone they know a helping hand. The point is that everybody needs to use their contacts at least to get started. Don't be afraid to plunder your own or your parents' telephone book. However, remember that getting in is only the start of what is a very long haul.

My real advice to anyone after a career in the City is this: think very carefully. Do you really want to work in the City? If you do, then go and do something else first. Become a lawyer. Become an accountant. Go out and work in industry and become a specialist in one sector. Work out exactly which part of an investment bank you want to be in and focus on getting there. Remember: there are bear markets as well as bull markets, and it is always useful to have a vocational qualification to fall back on if times are tough. There is nothing worse than being a washed-up 45-year-old banker or stockbroker qualified for nothing.

Chapter 2

Surviving on the Trading Floor

Surviving on
the Trading Floor

THE TRADING FLOOR WILL BE a familiar sight to those of you who work in the City, and to many who do not, because so many television interviews are beamed directly from trading floors. I presume it appeals to television producers – it's more interesting than just a talking head.

What do all those people sitting in rows staring at screens actually do? Why is it necessary to have them all in one room?

It's a pretty unpleasant working environment to get used to if, as I was, you have been accustomed to having your own office. There is barely any room. Even if you are prepared to have personal conversations on the telephone (and beware, they are all taped – see Chapter 5), there's no getting away from the fact that you are within inches of people on either side and they will hear every word. There is no room for personal possessions; the best you might manage is a photo of your children (or horse or dog) taped to your screen. You usually have only one (small) set of drawers. For someone as untidy as me, it is a real challenge.

Try asking one of these people what they are doing and they will probably say 'thousands of different things'. At the micro level that is true. Trading floors all vary; people in, say, Morgan Stanley may be doing totally different things on one trading floor to others within the same firm, let alone in comparison with those at another bank such as Merrill Lynch. No two trading floors are the same. However, what happens is not that difficult to explain at a macro level. Everyone sitting on a trading floor is doing (or supporting someone else doing) one of three things. They are either client-facing, risk-taking or analysing – and possibly all three.

Client-facing people are there specifically to track down potential clients – people with pools of money (or sometimes people who need money) – and persuade them that the best way to invest it would be through something that the bank can assist with. They are essentially a glorified telesales operation (and in fact they are called salespeople). If you were trying to justify their overpaid existence, you could argue that it is hard to find clients, that they need to build up relationships with them over the long term, that it takes someone with an intimate understanding of how clients work to do the job properly. In the old days (say twenty years ago) these people were the kings of the trading floor; they would call a fund manager client, chat about the day's news, help the client decide what to buy or sell, and then carry out the client's instructions. The client would pay a commission on the trade, which before 1986 used to be a fixed fee. It's not unlike buying a coffee at Starbucks, except when you buy a coffee you look at the tariff on the wall – a cappuccino costs x and a latte y. You wouldn't think of saying to the barista, 'Look here, I buy at least three cups of coffee a day here, so how about a discount for bulk purchases? I have to warn you that if you don't agree, I will be moving my coffee-purchasing activities to Coffee Republic down the street.'

Now a cup of coffee is a physical product and it may be convenient to buy it in Starbucks because it is near your office. You wouldn't walk fifty yards out of your way just to save a few pence. But trading floors are not selling a physical product and a few pence off each transaction adds up to a whole lot of money. So fund managers – the trading floor's clients – do flex their buying muscles. The job of the client-facing people on a trading floor is to give these clients more or less of whatever service they wish, so as to maximise the chances of making some money from them.

But however much fund managers flex their muscles to negotiate lower broking commissions, corporate finance and its associated functions remain to this day an area where price competition is notably lacking. This is not a criticism, it is a fact. If a company is listed on the UK Stock Exchange then it must meet a list of requirements, including having an established track record, suitable accounting standards, and so on. It is also required to have a sponsor, which has to be selected from an approved list. There is a lesser stock market in the UK, the Alternative Investment Market, designed for smaller and less well-established companies. The requirements to list on AIM include the appointment of a nominated adviser. In both cases the advisers liaise with the stock exchange to ensure that the rules and regulations are adhered to. For a company preparing to list its shares for the first time, this will necessitate many long hours working with the investment bank or stockbroker acting as its sponsor or nominated adviser. Relationships built during that time will not be easily discarded once the company's shares are trading. You can imagine that when it comes to doing deals these companies are far more likely to stick with the people they know and trust than to start shopping around on the basis of price.

This contrasts sharply with the situation in the USA, where a company deals directly with the stock exchange on which it is listed and is far more responsible for its own actions, unable to hide behind advisers. Here transaction-based relationships and price are much more important. Mind you, these things are all relative, and companies coming to the stock market for the first time still tend to pay 7 per cent of whatever money they raise, which for a company of any size is quite an exorbitant amount.

Thus in the UK the City is (to misquote the Lawrence Report) institutionally anti-competitive. This allows for a regular stream of what economists would call super-normal profits. And this directly accounts for the pay disparity between people working there and people working in the real world.

* * *

Salesmen can be selling different things to different clients. If the salesman on the floor is marketing the bank's knowledge and understanding of the share market, he or she will typically be talking to people managing pools of money for pension funds or insurance companies, and not to people managing pools of money in central banks. However, on another part of the trading floor, or on a different trading floor, there will be someone else talking to central bankers about, say, government bonds, and so on.

The second group of people on a trading floor are those taking risks on behalf of their employer. These are traders.

They are essentially making decisions to buy or sell things in the hope that they will be able to sell or buy them later at a 'margin' – in other words a profit. This is what Nick Leeson was doing (or what the Barings management thought he was doing). The number of different things it is possible to buy and sell is limited only by the imagination of people working in the City (arguably they should therefore be very limited). So you can buy and sell ordinary stocks and shares and government debt, as well as more exotic-sounding items such as asset-backed securities, fixed income derivatives or junk bonds. This is not a textbook and I am not going to explain what these are; suffice it to say that they are all financial instruments that have been invented by someone somewhere who had more times on their hands than I did to dream them up.

All that traders are doing is betting, using someone else's money. You might be persuaded that with all the information available to them they have an especially reliable form book and therefore the odds should be reduced, but don't believe a word of it. If someone tells you they are a trader, ask them what they trade and also what their limits are. Anyone who goes to the bookie's usually limits their bets. If you don't, and put a large sum on an unfavoured horse, it is the kind of mistake you make only once unless you have an understanding partner. It is the same in the City – exceeding your trading limit is a mistake that you make only once unless you have an understanding employer.

The third group of people on a trading floor are reviewing all manner of information and distilling it in a form that is supposedly relevant and useful to the managers of the pools of money who are their clients. This may range from a review of the world stock markets to the prospects for interest rates, the performance of the American economy, or indeed the prospects of an individual company such as BP or Shell. In theory, fund managers haven't got time to assemble every piece of information available and work out what it means, so investment banks helpfully employ some supposedly quite clever people to do it for them. This is all part of the service. The theory is that all this wisdom pouring from the keyboards of the commentators (variously called analysts, economists or strategists – all performing slightly different variations on the theme) assists the clients in deciding what to buy, sell or hold in their pools of investments.

All three groups of people on an equities trading floor could be described as stockbrokers, because they buy and sell (or advise on buying or selling, or make it possible to buy and sell) company shares for clients who have money and want to invest it. My initial job on the trading floor was, as I have said earlier, as a 'specialist salesperson', meaning that I was effectively in two of the three camps described above; I was described as specialist because I was attached to a team of investment analysts who specialised in one industrial sector, but I did relatively little analysis, focusing instead on calling fund managers, as a general equity salesperson might, to apprise them of investment (or disinvestment) ideas. A generalist could be calling about any ideas; my calls were restricted to the sector I was attached to. I spent the first nine months sitting in the research department and the next nine months sitting on the sales desk, so I really did see how both places worked.

Despite my disastrous interview with the misogynist salesman on my way into the City, I did learn one very useful thing from him, which helped me survive on a trading floor for as long as I did. During the interview he asked me what the purpose of working on a trading floor was. I can't remember my answer but I do remember what *he* thought it should have been – the sole purpose of being there, he said, whether you are talking to the client, taking risks or analysing data, is to help the client make money. If the client's investment performance is good, he or she will be happy, and you will have done your job well.

So all three groups of people work together in order to help the fund management client grow his or her pools of money. The salesperson will talk to the client and help him decide what to buy or sell, using the research that the analysts have churned out. Then, when he has decided, the traders will facilitate his trade. Not rocket science, is it?

* * *

My first day on a trading floor in the City didn't augur well. I arrived to start my apprenticeship to the Arrogant Twosome, and was immediately directed to a desk several metres away but within sight of them. The only communication I had with them all day was when the more senior one came up to my desk and gave me a list of fund management clients who had been invited to attend a company presentation the following Tuesday, after the company in question had published its half-year results. My task was to ring them all up and ask whether they were going to come or not. This was really going to test my MBA!

Ostensibly, the purpose of the presentation was to assist the fund management clients to get to know the company better, give them an opportunity to question the management, and generally help them decide whether or not to buy, sell or continue to hold the company's shares. The bank did of course have a relationship with the company – it was a client of the corporate broking department. Corporate broking clients are not managers of money, but publicly quoted companies such as this to which the bank provided advice.

The purpose of the meeting was therefore public relations. The bank's task was to make sure that as many people as possible were drafted in to listen to the chief executive and the finance director of the company make presentations. If attendance was poor, the bank could expect to receive quite a lot of criticism from the company. Later I discovered what everyone who has worked in the City for more than five minutes learns immediately; if not enough people turn up, then you walk round the trading floor imposing a three-line whip so that the presentation room looks full. The odds are that the company will not be able to distinguish a trading-floor salesperson or trader from a fund manager anyway.

So I spent my first morning on the trading floor ringing up complete strangers – a good introduction to what was to come. Admittedly, I couldn't be given any real work to do; as I hadn't yet passed my Securities and Futures Authority (SFA) examinations, I wasn't allowed to actually communicate any investment ideas to anyone. Around one o'clock, I looked up from my desk. The Arrogant Twosome, who sat facing each other right next to the main part of the trading floor, close enough to catch each other's grunts but far enough away to be able to practise hurling scrunched-up paper balls at each other, had vanished. I'd been there for four hours and no one had shown me where the lavatory or the coffee machine were or even asked me to lunch. Suddenly I knew what it felt like to be in the loneliest place in the world.

Oh well, I thought. It's obviously a busy day for them. No doubt they will get round to asking me to lunch tomorrow. How wrong could I be? The next day came and went much like the first, with a list of tasks deposited on my desk at the beginning of the day and the minimum of breath wasted on giving me instructions. They were off for the rest of the day again. I sat in isolated splendour, trying to work out exactly what I was supposed to do. Once again, no one came near me all day, and nobody asked me to lunch.

That weekend I reflected on my start in the City. I hadn't entered with a lot of graduates, who would at least have had each other for company and been on a formal training programme. I had started out completely from scratch, working for two men for whom I had clearly been a second choice. It was hardly surprising that they weren't rushing to ask me out to lunch. Their job was to write investment analysis on companies, pointing out valuation anomalies and recommending which stocks to buy and sell. My job was simply to make them famous – not in the *Hello!* sense, but famous with the money managers of the world.

Things got marginally better after I was sent on a week's course as part of my SFA. This consisted of sitting in a classroom somewhere near the Edgware Road all day long and then answering practice questions in the evening, followed by an examination at the London Stock Exchange. I sat in front of a computer screen and clicked on the answers to a whole series of multiple-choice questions. The vast majority related to information that had taken me a week to assemble and would take me less than a day to forget – how many days' settlement were needed to trade a Japanese bond, how many stocks were in the Hang Seng, and how many days' notice you had to give a private client to pull out of a written advisory agreement. Then as now the bulk of the examination was taken up with regulation.

Once I had passed my exams the Arrogant Twosome let me progress to organising the numbers on the front of their published research notes. This at least involved the operation of a spreadsheet, and now I could demonstrate I was good for something. Yet I still couldn't shake off the stigma of not being the girl they had really wanted.

I was determined to work my way into the affections of these two men. They were very close friends, although very different, and aged about fifteen years apart. They had once written investment research on the same industrial sector but were now covering a different sector each, splitting a third sector between them. Before they would let me represent them on the phone to clients, I would have to earn their trust.

Both men had the most extraordinarily untidy desks, particularly the elder. I took it upon myself to stay late every night and come in every weekend to try to put his desk into some semblance of order. This was not an altruistic move, or even a purely sycophantic one – in the process I hoped to learn something about the companies that he followed. Instead of just taking company information and putting it in the appropriate file I would make sure I read it before I did so, and even read several pages back in the file to which the information was allotted. Thus I learnt how these companies had come to be the organisations they now were. Every company has a history in terms of what it has divested, who it has acquired, when and why – the financial milestones of its life. With cricket now well into its off-season I was able to spend Saturday and Sunday afternoons wading through piles of paper while Mr M obligingly looked after son number one at home. To ingratiate myself further, I even spent hours loading my boss's lists of personal investments into his personal organiser so that he could easily keep an eye on how they were performing.

But what of the more junior member of the Arrogant Twosome? How was I ever going to win him round? His desk and filing system didn't need me; before I had even arrived he had been allocated, much to his disgust, the most blue-blooded of the previous year's graduate intake as his junior analyst. She had even – shock horror! – been a debutante. So appalled was he by how posh she was that he sat her even farther away from him than he did me.

It took me a while to discover this girl's existence, but once I did I realised that she was probably the Most Socially Accept-able Girlfriend I was ever going to have. She had a genuinely posh pedigree, having grown up in a large house set among thousands of acres and having attended the same school as the Queen of Denmark. Her brothers, father and many other relatives had been to Eton, and there was even a family title, which her eldest brother would probably one day inherit. But she also had a brain, and her interest in the stock market was a genuine and abiding one. Much later, when I met her family, I realised that MSAG had inherited her strong commercial judgement from her father, who, having been saddled with a large house and many acres from an early age, had astutely worked to build the family fortune back to a level where all this could be sustained without having to endure the trials of opening the family home to the public. MSAG never gave any of this away, and was a model of humility, beavering away in the far corner of the trading floor.

Having billeted MSAG at a safe distance from him, the younger of the Arrogant Twosome delegated to her all his number-crunching, filing, list-making and background research. She wasn't encouraged to come to his desk, but he occasionally dropped by hers, or telephoned her to issue instructions. Her desk was also the closest to the RNS machine – the Regulatory News Service of the London Stock Exchange. This device was then the only source of all information emanating from the Stock Exchange, including all company announcements, which were required to be issued first to the Stock Exchange for onward transmission. So MSAG was able to keep an eye on the companies that the younger of the Arrogant Twosome followed and sprint to his desk with anything that needed delivering in a hurry. Once I discovered MSAG, I knew that not only had I found a friend, I had also identified an ally. Like me, she hadn't been her superior's first choice. And also like me, she was going to have to win him round if she was going to succeed.

My real breakthrough with this young man (who was younger than me) came when he got engaged. We were all delighted for him and rushed off to buy champagne. By this time I had started talking to fund managment clients and was anxious for the Twosome to write as many research notes as possible, so that I had something to talk about on the telephone. Unfortunately, as the wedding approached my young boss became more preoccupied with organising the arrangements and seemed less and less enthusiastic about writing research. This left me at my desk drumming my fingers, wondering how I was ever going to get him to become more productive. Finally I put it to him that we might usefully exchange duties. If I organised the logistics of the wedding, he would be able to use his time to write investment research for me to market to the fund managers that I was convinced were just waiting for the pearls of wisdom to fall from his lips, or even his keyboard. That way we would both be fully occupied, and while he was on honeymoon I would have something to do.

This seemed to be an acceptable arrangement, and so I found myself organising the cars to take the bridesmaids to the reception as well as all his honeymoon flights and hotel bookings. You could be forgiven for thinking that this was rather ridiculous – why did I bother with an MBA if my job was to organise hotel and flight bookings? But the truth is that it was undoubtedly an earnings-enhancing decision for the shareholders of the bank. As a result of having this administrative burden lifted from his shoulders, my youthful boss wrote research as never before. To this day he is regarded as arguably the brightest and the best investment analyst in the City of London. And anything that freed up his time, allowing him to concentrate on value-added activities, was surely in everyone's interest.

In fact I lost count of the menial tasks I performed for these two while I was there. I certainly got their dry cleaning on more than one occasion, was frequently dispatched to collect their lunches, booked restaurants, nights at the theatre and flowers for their wives. This makes it sound as though I was a glorified secretary, but I assure you I happily did all those things in order to get the boys to concentrate on what they were really supposed to be doing.

* * *

Meanwhile, what was *I* really supposed to be doing? My job, as a specialist salesperson, was to ring up fund managers (the clients with the pools of money) and alert them to the latest bons mots falling from the pens of my two bosses. As I said earlier, I was a hybrid of telesales team member and analyst.

I needed to impress on these fund managers how terribly clever my bosses were, how well they knew their sector, how insightful their views were – indeed, how indispensable their services were if the fund manager was to make an informed decision about which shares to buy or sell. Active fund management, where the fund manager actively takes investment decisions rather than letting a computer allocate money between shares, has quarterly milestone measurements. At the end of each quarter the fund's performance is measured against whatever benchmark they are using. Thus the purpose of my telephone calls to clients was to provide information that would enable them to out-perform the market.

Eighty per cent of money under management is probably in the hands of 20 per cent of a stockbroker's clients, and those 20 per cent need first-class servicing and very careful handling. In our case they would normally receive direct personal phone calls from the Arrogant Twosome, and wouldn't deign to talk to me. However, fund managers of that size usually have their own research departments, and while my bosses spoke to the fund managers themselves I would be developing a relationship with the analyst on the 'buy side' (as clients managing pools of money are typically known). Every month, with the approval of my bosses, I would be issued with a list of fund management clients that had to be called and a recommendation as to the frequency with which I should be calling them. I had to make a record of these calls and every month I had to hand it in, like a time sheet.

If I hadn't called a client as frequently as I should, an explanation would be required. It was never good enough to say, 'He's not interested in hearing from us, he doesn't rate either of the Arrogant Twosome and he has no time for what they've got to say.' I was expected to return to the fray the following month and try again.

I vividly remember one particular client, working at County NatWest Investment Management (which no longer exists as such). Supposedly a target of the elder of the Arrogant Twosome, he never came to company presentations, never gave us good marks on any measurement criteria, and certainly never directed any commission in our direction. Every month I would go through the ritual of leaving a message on his answerphone, and every month he would fail to return it. If I had had e-mail in those days, I could have added to my bombardment by sending him witty comments through cyberspace. I doubt he would have taken much notice of those either.

One day I did actually get through to him; the conversation went something like this:

'Hello, it's Mrs Moneypenny from Eurobank.'

'Yes.'

'I just wondered if you would be interested in hearing my bosses' views on XYZ plc.'

'No.' (Very loquacious, this client.)

'Why not?'

'Because as far as I'm concerned you've got nothing interesting to say.'

Rejection is never easy, whether from a lover or a client. I am not sure what my response should have been to this but after months of having come up against a brick wall I finally lost my temper. So the conversation continued:

'How do you know I've got nothing to say and no value to add if you won't even listen to me in the first place? I think it's absolutely outrageous that you can make a pronouncement like that on the basis of no evidence whatsoever. If you had any decency at all you would at least agree to meet me for lunch to see whether you find any sense at all in our investment views. At least if you did that, and then told me I had got nothing useful to say and no value to add, I would assume you had done it on the basis of having reviewed the evidence!'

I held my breath, knowing that I had overstepped the mark and wondering how on earth I was going to explain this away when yet another month went past without any communication with this man. I didn't see how any of what I had just said was in any way going to address the poor image he clearly already had of us. Imagine my surprise, therefore, when he responded: 'Yes, OK, that seems like a reasonable suggestion. How about lunch in the tapas bar in Leadenhall Market next Thursday?'

Thus started a long and commercially successful relationship between me and the bolshy client at County NatWest. He became such a wonderful client that I even flew back from Hong Kong in 1995 to take him to a big industry function, the annual fund management beanfeast at the Grosvenor House known as the Analysts' Dinner.

So now you know. Trading floors are not complicated places, and surviving on one is really not that hard. You have to learn to have no pride of authorship, to give due deference to the egos around you, and to realise that you are all there for one main purpose – to help your clients, the investment managers of the universe, make money. If there is a secondary purpose, it is to allow your non-trading-floor colleagues to look good in front of *their* clients, the public companies whose growth and sustainment are possible through the miracle of the world's capital markets. You should have tenacity, the capacity to work long hours and the ability to place no limits on how far you will sink to please your employers or your clients. Quite simple, really.

'It's easy to succeed in this game,' MSAG once told me. 'You just have to use the chocolate knickers treatment where you can. It almost unfailingly works with male clients.' What, I asked, was the chocolate knickers treatment? 'It's quite simple,' she said in a very matter-of-fact voice. 'You just have to look at every client as though they are wearing chocolate knickers that you would like to lick off.'

Chapter 3

The Money-go-round

The Money-go-round

ONCE LOST HALF A MILLION pounds in a single lunchtime. No, I didn't leave it in my handbag in a restaurant. The money disappeared because I came back later than I should have done from a client lunch. It is fair to say that the incident was insignificant considering the trillions of pounds that are moved around the City each day, and the purpose of this chapter is to explain at least partially how this movement works. If this is a book on survival, then regard this chapter as describing the terrain within which you need to survive, rather than the core of the survival technique itself. My lunchtime disaster is used merely as an illustration, and if you already know how the theory works you may care to skip to the practical, as it were, on page 50.

What do all the many different organisations that make up the City do? Why is it necessary to have so many of them? Let me say here and now that everything I am going to say in this chapter will be a gross simplification, but one that will allow any reader to understand the world I inhabited during my time in the City.

If you work in the Square Mile I can almost guarantee that the bit you work in seems to you by far the most important. But how do you define 'most important'? Some City activities get the most publicity, some are handling the largest amounts of money, and some are the most profitable. All of them are playing their part in moving money from place to place. This might seem a mindless activity, but it is more common than you think. Everyone takes part somewhere along the line.

Joe Bloggs, for example, is an average bloke living in an ordinary town somewhere in an ordinary part of England. He works for a building contractor and they pay very well. He owns his own house, having long ago paid off his mortgage, and saves regularly for his retirement. A lot of the money he saves he puts into his pension fund, and the rest of it he puts in the building society. The building society in which he is saving his money pays him interest. How do they get the money to pay him his interest? They lend the money he deposits with them to John Smith, another ordinary bloke living in an ordinary town somewhere in England. John Smith has borrowed the money from the building society to buy a house. As it happens, the building contractor that built the development, from whom John Smith buys the house, is in fact the same company that employs Joe Bloggs. They use the money that John Smith has just paid them for the house to pay Joe Bloggs's salary. He then saves some of that in the building society, and off we go again.

The City of London is really no different. It is just that the flow of money occurs within an even tighter circle than the one described above. Whereas Joe Bloggs and John Smith may live hundreds of miles apart, in the City it is more likely that the money going round in circles is passing between people located not only in the same geographical area but possibly in the same building, and sometimes even in the same company.

All this money in circulation will at some point be invested in one or more of the following areas: cash, property, part-ownership of companies, part-ownership of debt, or funds that invest in all of them. In City jargon these are known as different 'asset classes'.

If you are looking after a pool of money you first have to decide how to divide the money up between the different asset classes – what proportion to hold as cash, what proportion to invest in property, and so on. That's half the battle, and once again there's jargon to describe this process – asset allocation.

In the UK most invested money is in shares, so let's see what shares are all about.

If you own a share in ICI or Microsoft, you own a very small part of that company. By definition it is a very small piece because in the case of ICI there are 1.2 billion shares on issue and in the case of Microsoft about 10.7 billion. Also, in the case of Microsoft, Bill Gates owns rather a lot of the shares personally. So owning one share isn't really going to give you any say in how Bill Gates runs the company. Owning shares in a company does, however, entitle you to receive a percentage of the profits that it makes. Every year, a company's directors decide how much, if any, of the profits to give to the company's owners – this is the dividend. You will therefore receive whatever dividend they decide to give you. Your shares will also entitle you to a vote, in proportion to the importance of your shareholding, on major decisions affecting the company, such as appointments to the board of directors and its choice of auditors.

In the case of Microsoft, they have up until now elected to keep all the company's profits within the company. Shareholders thus benefited from the share price going up, but did not enjoy an income stream.

The majority of shares in both the United Kingdom and the United States are in the hands of 'institutional investors', in other words organisations, rather than individuals, that invest money professionally, staffed by people who invest money for a living. I usually describe these companies and their staff as the 'professional investment community'. In many cases computers make the investment decisions by analysing past statistics and then allocating money according to the results. Fortunately the largest proportion of money under management is still in the hands of people, so-called 'active' investors. For most of my time in the City, these were my clients.

Company shares can either be publicly traded – in other words anyone can buy and sell them across a stock exchange – or privately held. If a company's shares are privately held then they can only be bought and sold by individual arrangement between the buyer and the seller. These transactions are infrequent, and you have to find a buyer and seller who wish to transact at the same time and at a price they both agree on. Fund managers do invest in privately owned companies, but as these are investments they cannot easily get out of they are more risky. They are known as 'venture capital' or 'private equity', and account for a relatively small proportion of the pools of money. If Joe Bloggs retires and the company managing his pension fund has invested all his money in a private company, and cannot find a buyer for the shares, Joe will be unable to draw his pension. He may not be very amused.

So the vast proportion of shares in which fund managers invest are in public companies. The question is: where do these fund managers get their ideas about what companies to invest in? One of the principal sources are the occupants of the trading floors who talk to them, the 'sell side'. Trading floors that specialise in shares (as opposed to any other type of financial instrument or asset class) are also called equities trading floors, as shares are frequently referred to as equities. The occupants of a trading floor specialising in equities can also be referred to as stockbrokers, because they broke (i.e. sell) stocks (i.e. shares) to clients (i.e. fund managers).

Stockbrokers have three essential sides to their operation. In no particular order they are: a research department, which analyses the profits of companies and attempts to value what they are really worth, and is are tasked with coming up with interesting investment opportunities and ideas; salespeople, essentially key account managers, whose job is to stay in touch with the fund managers and keep them informed of the bright ideas the research department is coming up with; and the traders, whose job, once the fund manager has decided what he wishes to buy and sell, is to actually make the deals happen – in other words, the three elements of the trading floor described in Chapter 2.

These three components form the backbone of the so-called 'secondary' operation in any investment bank – secondary not because it is secondary in importance, but because its main business is to buy and sell shares that have already been issued. When a company lists (or 'floats') on the Stock Exchange for the first time and issues new shares to people wanting to buy them – as, for example, BT did when it was privatised – this is known as a primary market transaction because it is the first time these shares have existed. Once they do exist, and can be bought and sold by people every day, they are considered to be part of the secondary market, because the people buying and selling them are the second (and third and fourth, etc.) people to own them. The day-to-day business of the three sections of the trading floor is to conduct secondary market operations – i.e. buy and sell shares – on behalf of their clients, the world's fund managers.

Sitting somewhere else in the same organisation, probably not very far from the trading floor, will be a group of people whose principal job is to advise public companies on how to finance their growth. This particular lot can be arbitrarily grouped together as corporate finance, although in practice there are people with different functions within corporate finance, including merger and acquisition specialists, corporate brokers and structured finance teams.

Of course, corporate finance and the three components of the equity trading floor frequently work together. Let's say that the corporate finance department of an investment bank has among its clients a company that manufactures drugs on a global basis and makes stonking profits. Megapharmaceutical plc wishes to buy a tiny little bio-technology company in Switzerland. The corporate finance team advising it suggests that they should issue some new shares to pay for this purchase. The investment research department – part of the trading floor, essentially active in the secondary market – will then write a piece of research that extols the merits of this tiny little bio-technology company, and shows how the profits of Megapharmaceutical would be substantially enhanced were they to buy it. This piece of research will then be taken up by another part of the trading floor, the sales desk, and pitched to fund managers over the telephone, probably supported by an in-person presentation from the CEO of Megapharmaceutical. If the fund manager likes the story, he or she will then buy some of the new shares that Megapharmaceutical is issuing to raise the money to pay for the acquisition. If they don't, they may well sell some or all of the Megapharmaceutical shares they already own.

* * *

Does my recommendation mean much to you? Now that I am a columnist on a national newspaper it probably counts for something, but ten years ago, when I was a humble investment analyst, I doubt you would have been very interested in what I thought about anything. Indeed, my recollection is that the only people who were very interested in what I thought about individual stocks and shares in those days were taxi drivers.

'So, love, what do you do for a crust?'

'Actually, I'm a stockbroker.'

'Oh, what shares do you recommend? Vodafone looks cheap.'

'I'm not really able to comment – I only have a licence to advise professional investors.'

'Come on, you must have punted a few yourself.'

'I'm sorry to disappoint you, but I don't invest in shares directly myself, I put my money in managed funds.'

'Pull the other one. You just don't want us all to be as rich as you, isn't that it? What shares should I be buying?'

'Well, if you must invest in shares, my advice is to invest in something that you know a bit about. What are the prospects for the taxi business?'

(Many guffaws from the cabbie.) 'Not good, love, we've a recession on.'

'We haven't got a recession on. The technical definition of a recession is two successive quarters of negative GDP growth and the last two quarters actually showed positive growth, admittedly of modest proportions . . .'

And so on until either I told him to short Manganese Bronze Holdings or we arrived at our destination.

Offering share recommendations was once an issue for my Most Glamorous Girlfriend – or rather a friend of hers. MGG was a wonderful asset while I was working in the City; she accompanied me to many client functions and played golf with several clients long before Mr M ever took up the sport. She even scored at a client cricket match! I secured her support for these occasions by promising her access to a whole range of solvent single men. MGG had enjoyed a brief 'starter marriage' to a former colleague of Mr M's, and I felt so guilty about the fact that it hadn't worked out that I felt compelled to find her a replacement.

Both colleagues and clients were interviewed by MGG, some for longer than others. One colleague of mine managed to retain her affections for quite a while, and she even took him to a work function of her own one night. In those days MGG worked for a prestigious advertising agency in Berkeley Square, part of Sir Martin Sorrell's WPP empire. Her beau made the mistake of having a few drinks too many before turning up at MGG's event, and so was rather the worse for wear when introduced to her boss, the agency's chief executive. 'So what do you do?' said the boss. 'Um, I'm a stockbroker,' came the reply. The boss's next question was predictable. 'So, then, what shares should I be buying?' When drunk, it is even more important to stick to offering the advice that people should buy shares in businesses they understand. Thus MGG's boyfriend proffered the suggestion that her boss should acquire some shares in WPP, then trading at 51p. This went down very badly. 'Don't be ridiculous,' said MGG's boss, 'I already have a garage full at £2.' As it turned out, although he was substantially over the alcohol limit for providing investment advice, this was probably the best call this particular stockbroker ever made. MGG's boss should have piled in at 51p and averaged out the cost of his investment. Even today, in the throes of a bear market, WPP shares trade at c. £3.70.

* * *

Eliot Laurence Spitzer is a New York District Attorney who would be quite interested in what my recommendation was on individual shares were I still in the employ of an investment bank. Equity analysts, as I explained earlier, are people who review the information (financial and otherwise) available on public companies and attempt to value them. If this value intimates a lower or higher price than that at which the company is currently trading, then a recommendation is made to buy or sell the shares. Mr Spitzer's contention is that analysts frequently issue a 'buy' recommendation when they don't believe a share to be a 'buy' at all, but where the company is currently an important client of the corporate finance division of their employer. In other words, conflicts of interest militate against the provision of truly independent advice.

So how independent – or otherwise – is investment research? As we have seen, while an equity trading floor has fund managers as its clients, the corporate finance department has a different sort of client altogether – publicly quoted companies. The money made by the corporate finance department from underwriting the issue of equities, and corporate finance advice, is usually much greater than commission from trading shares on the secondary market. The corporate client is a very important source of income in any bank, particularly as they are usually letting the bank arrange all sorts of financing for them – bonds, loans, treasury products, etc. In just the same way, you and I are more valuable to our local bank when they start to sell us insurance, pensions and the like – in fact, if they are only providing us with a current account and no other service it is very unlikely that they are making any money out of us at all. The more products they can sell to clients the better.

So you can see that corporate clients are very important. It is hardly surprising that the status of a company (whether client or potential client) may affect an investment bank's decision as to whether or not to recommend a 'sell' on their shares. Critics argue that this massively compromises the independence of investment research. The truth is that when I became a stockbroker it was never a written-down rule that you couldn't recommend a sell on a corporate stock. The fact that the company was a corporate client of the bank was disclosed on the front page of every piece of research, and it was generally accepted that our clients (i.e. the fund managers) knew that if we put a 'hold' recommendation on a corporate stock that effectively meant sell. MSAG, when a graduate trainee, asked outright whether it was possible to put a sell on a corporate stock and was answered in a way that made it clear that while she was free to do what she wished, such a move wouldn't be very clever. Thus there was no explicit direction to refrain from recommending a sell, but there was a tacit understanding that it wasn't done and would be seriously frowned upon. To survive in the City, I was told, you must never put a 'sell' or even a 'reduce' recommendation on the shares of a company to whom your employer is a retained – i.e. paid – adviser. Eliot Spitzer, welcome to the real world.

Actually, it would be a good thing if everyone were to write honest recommendations, and set target share prices that they believed, in their research. Stockbrokers would gain a lot of credibility with the fund management industry, which has to stomach useless and biased research notes a lot of the time. The higher the credibility a stockbroker has with a fund manager, the more stock they will be able to place with him. If you know that someone never sells you a dodgy story, then when they ring up and tell you they are bringing a company to the market and are offering you shares, you are much more likely to take them up. I am reminded of the fact that my mother goes over sixty miles to buy her electrical goods because the shop in question has never sold her a dummy. Nothing she has bought there has ever broken down. That would be the ideal relationship for any stockbroker to build with its fund manager client base, and would also serve the interests of the corporate client when they came to issue shares. But of course it is all far too altruistic, and never really happens.

* * *

When you look at all this money being pushed around from place to place it is easy to understand how I was once able to lose half a million pounds one lunchtime. I was a junior analyst and specialist salesperson working in the research department of an investment bank, and I was one of the people charged with analysing and valuing certain UK public companies and coming up with investment ideas to pitch to the clients. Together with my then boss, the elder of the Arrogant Twosome, I was responsible for following the fortunes of, and being 'an expert' on, a big UK-headquartered multinational company. Its principal competitor was based in the United States. We were a particularly small investment bank at the time and didn't actually cover any United States companies, so we only kept a watching eye on the competitor to see how and when any of its moves would have an impact on the company that we followed.

I arrived at work at the usual 7.15 a.m. In my day that gave you a few minutes to read the papers before the day's announcements started to spew out of the printer. If you were an analyst following the fortunes of a company whose results were out that day, you would stand by the machine, snatch the pages away and retire to your desk to quickly assimilate the news and formulate a view on what it might mean for the share price. Then you would gather near the floor microphone just before 7.50, ready to tell the entire trading floor what those views were.

We called this speaking 'on the shout', and it is a pretty daunting experience when you do it for the first time. No hush descends on the audience; they carry on doing whatever they were before – talking on telephones, rustling papers, getting up and walking around the room, drinking coffee, and so on. When I first joined the bank I was whisked off for some 'shout training' with a man who taught me to think about my message as though it were a headline in the *Daily Mirror*. His contention was that the leader writers and financial journalists on the *Mirror* were far harder working than their peers on the broadsheets because they had to condense a challenging story into a few short words comprehensible to people with average intellect and limited vocabulary – in other words, equity salesmen.

What equity salesmen really want is for their analysts to be endowed with a crystal ball. I could have certainly done with one that day. My team were planning a relaxed day; it was a Friday, and none of our companies had results due out. The Arrogant Twosome both had lunches booked and so did the market maker on the 'leader book', i.e. the trader who was in charge of the biggest and most liquid shares, which included the multinational company we were responsible for analysing.

These days these circumstances would never have arisen, because shares in the largest companies are now bought and sold through the SETS™, the London Stock Exchange's electronic blue chip market where the 200 most liquid shares are traded. This operates like a gigantic electronic marketplace, where people put their buy and sell requests up on the screen, along with the price and quantity they require, and these are considered firm bids/offers. The system then matches the orders and clears them, generating the paperwork automatically. It's like putting up a notice on the Internet saying that you want to buy a new TV, specifying the exact make and model and the maximum price you are prepared to pay, as well as quoting your credit card details. This is a binding offer on your part. Some unseen search engine then trawls the Net to find someone who has exactly this TV to sell at or below the price you have stipulated. You awake the next day to find the TV on your doorstep and your credit card debited, and the receipt duly arrives in the post. You can see from the receipt where you bought it.

In 1993 we were a long way from that. In those days a client would ring up and say that he (or she) wanted to sell some shares. For example, they might wish to sell 100,000 shares in Tesco. All brokers who traded (or 'made a market') in Tesco shares would have indicators on their screens specifying at what approximate prices they would be prepared to buy or sell those shares, and in what quantity, but in order to find a firm price offer for a specific volume a client would have to call around a few brokers. From my perspective then, the dialogue would go something like this:

Client (on telephone to limited-vocabulary equity salesman in my office): 'Harry, could you get me a price in 100,000 Tesco?' (Note: sensible client declines to tell Harry whether he wishes to buy or sell these 100,000 Tesco shares.)

Harry (having put the client on hold, or more likely having put his hand over the telephone) shouts to the person making markets in food retailing stocks: 'Clive, can you make me a price in 100,000 Tesco?'

Clive: '420 440.' (Note: traders have an even more limited vocabulary than salespeople; in fact, the ones I knew mostly grunted. Whole sentences, when they did appear, would be delivered in a strong estuary accent.)

Harry (having taken hand off telephone): '420 440.' (Note: this indicates that the trader would be prepared to buy 100,000 shares from the client at £4.20 a share. Alternatively, he would be prepared to sell the client 100,000 shares in Tesco at £4.40 a share.)

Client: 'OK, I'll sell 100,000 Tesco at 420.'

Harry: 'Hang on a minute' (puts hand back over telephone). 'Clive! CLIVE! Schroders want to sell 100,000 Tesco at 420 – yes?'

Clive: (Noise sounding like assenting grunt.)

Harry (hand off telephone): 'No problems. You've sold us 100,000 Tesco at 420. Which account do you want me to book it to?'

And that's pretty well the end of the exchange. No paper-work changes hands immediately, and although Harry would have had to fill in a booking slip and send it off to the back office the client hadn't lifted a pen. Despite this, everyone knew that the next day the client would own 100,000 fewer shares in Tesco and would be £420,000 (less dealing costs) richer.

Of course, you might well ask whether the bank employing Harry and Clive really wanted to own 100,000 shares in Tesco. The answer is that of course they didn't – they fully intended to sell them on again as fast as possible for more than £4.20 a share, and book the profit. (Clive the trader calls the shares he currently owns – or owes – his 'book', and would be described in the above transaction as taking 100,000 Tesco 'onto the book'.)

What would be nice, needless to say, would be if Tesco then announced some wonderful piece of news so that every-one would be trying to buy shares – Clive would then put up the price to, say, £5, sell the shares to another of Harry's clients the same day, and the bank would have made a profit of 80p a share, or £80,000. All for a couple of telephone calls. Nice work if you can get it, eh?

The other side of the coin, though, is that Clive might be stuck with the shares and still own them at the end of the day. At that point he would have to find the money to pay for the shares – in practice borrowed from the parent bank – and the overnight interest charge. Even worse, the next day there still might not be a buyer, and in the end Clive would have to sell the shares for a loss at, say, £4 in order to get rid of them.

Returning to that sunny Friday in April, my boss and I noticed on our screens mid-morning that the major US competitor of the company we followed was planning an announcement that afternoon and would be holding a tele-conference call at 3 p.m. UK time. Having agreed to be back in time to be in on the call, we went our separate ways at lunch.

I met my client in a restaurant very near the office. He was a relatively junior fund manager in quite a small organisa-tion, and not exactly from a blue chip background. I was transfixed by his tie, which glistened in the sun that was streaming in through the window, and clearly was made of something derived from oil rather than any natural fibre. As we munched our way through the courses, we exhausted social pleasantries and then specific conversation about stocks and shares, finally turning to personal matters. How was his love life? I asked. Terrible, he replied. He just didn't seem to be able to find a girlfriend.

At this point, for some reason, I could contain myself no longer. Had he considered, I enquired, whether his choice of neckwear might be affecting his success rate? I hurriedly went on to explain that I myself, then a youthful 31, wouldn't dream of dating a man who wore polyester ties. The client looked rather taken aback. I summoned the (very pretty) wait-ress. What did she think of the tie? Wasn't it dreadful? Very diplomatically, she mumbled something about how it was fine but she had seen better.

That was it. Despite having been out of the office for more than an hour, I swept the client off to the nearest tie shop, where I selected a suitable tie personally, paid for it out of my own money (see the chapter on regulation) and insisted he put it on there and then. I remember it to this day – it sported yellow flying ducks on a navy background. I then wished him better luck in the romance stakes and returned to my desk, twenty minutes late.

Back at the office someone had managed to buy something more expensive than a tie. As I mentioned earlier, as well as my boss and I being out, the market maker on the leader stocks and his team had also all gone out for a spot of lunch. I should stress that traders didn't have lunches as a matter of course; although stock exchange trading hours were then 8.30 to 4.30 there was no lunch break, and the decisions that had to be taken were sufficiently critical that lunch was not encouraged. When we were moving into a new building in the late 1990s I sat on the management committee that ensured that canteens were designed as part of the trading floors; if a sandwich could be readily obtained in close proximity to their desks, we reckoned, then traders could spend the minimum amount of time away from their screens. So this was an exceptional day – business was slow, there were no major announcements expected, and we didn't make markets in any US stocks, so a prospective conference call later in the day from a company whose fortunes we did not even formally follow was no reason to stick around.

The market maker had arranged for a colleague to cover him on the off-chance that any client would be silly enough to want to do business on a sunny Friday lunchtime. This chap was also covering several other pitches and was an experienced hand, so there were no doubts that he would be able to cope.

However, the United States had been open for business for a while and inevitably news of the proposed conference call had led to much discussion all over the world about what it might portend. A management change, perhaps? The company concerned was a massive international organisation with thousands of employees, so it was inevitable that, a couple of hours before the appointed time, word was beginning to seep out. The rumour was that the company, fed up with losing market share in its main market, was planning to slash the price of its flagship product.

Clearly this would be bad news for its competitors, including the company that my boss and I were supposed experts in and whose share price we commented on regularly. But the rumour hadn't reached us, because we were at lunch (or, in my case, out buying ties). It had, however, reached one of our clients, who owned a lot of shares in this competitor company. He didn't want to be owning quite so many when the company had cut prices (and therefore profits) to match the Americans.

When the client called up it was just after 2 p.m. and he asked for a price in 500,000 shares. This was quite a large transaction as the price was then just over £6. However, the stock was regularly traded and very liquid, and there were lots of shares on issue. Hence it was treated as a 'leader' stock. The experienced hand covering the leader stocks over lunchtime looked for both my boss and me to see whether we could think of any reason why he shouldn't take the trade. Of course, neither of us was there, so we couldn't tell him about the looming conference call at 3 p.m. and its likely effect on the share price of all companies in the sector, if the rumour about price-cutting was true. He therefore ended up buying half a million shares in the company from the client at around £6, using about £3 million of the bank's money.

There are two things that you should know at this point. The first is that, as the junior executive, it was my job to be back at my desk immediately after lunch, not spending my time hanging around in tie shops. My boss was much more senior and therefore at liberty to stay out as long as he wished. The second is that, after my boss returned, we did dial into the conference call at 3 p.m. And yes, the announcement was that the US company was planning to cut the price of its flagship product that day by 40 per cent.

So large was this US company that the implied reduction in profits sent the share price down immediately, and also affected the share price of every company in the sector. Thus the company that my boss and I followed, 500,000 of whose shares the bank had just taken ownership of at a cost of £3 million, also suffered. In fact, within an hour the price of that company had fallen by £1, and our book was looking at a loss of – you've guessed it – half a million pounds.

Now this is real money. It belongs to the shareholders of the bank and we had effectively lost it for them. The only saving grace was that it was early April and the bank's financial year was a calendar one, so we had the rest of the year to make up the loss. But none of us felt very happy that day, least of all the market maker, who returned from lunch to find a massive hole in his position, which would undoubtedly affect his bonus.

I did, however, put this story to good use much later when travelling around the leading universities in the country, recruiting graduates – what other profession, I asked, would put you in a position where you could manage to help them lose £500,000 at lunchtime?

* * *

What can you learn about survival in the City from this experience? First, never let everyone go to lunch at the same time.

Second, appreciate the value of information – if the clients know more than you, it is hardly a fair trade. And last but not least – never try to help out with a client's love life.

But there's a larger lesson too: don't try to work outside your own theatre of operations. I was a stockbroker, not a marriage guidance counsellor or a dating agency. While I was trying to be all things to my client, the real business I should have been doing, which would have made the bank far more money (or rather, lost them far less money), went unheeded. Stick to your knitting. If you are a good corporate finance or M&A adviser, keep doing that and don't pretend that you know the secondary market as well as you do the primary one. If you are good at raising debt finance, don't think you can throw in some equity finance on the back of it. Be really, really good at what you do. Then do it – don't try to do something else.

Chapter 4

Salaried in the City

Salaried in the City

DOES A MILLION POUNDS SEEM like a lot of money to you? For many people in the City it doesn't – it's simply what they earn each year. At the time of writing, even a graduate with no experience straight from university will earn some £40,000 per year, enough to make some people's eyes water. Salaries in the City are the subject of heated debate around dinner tables and many other discussion forums. It is the one subject on which my Longest Standing Girlfriend can become completely worked up. What on earth do people do that enables them to command such a premium? she asks. Do they really make any contribution to society? Why are they not paid the same as a teacher in Lewisham? Surely teachers, nurses and doctors are all providing a much greater service to society than stockbrokers?

There is no moral justification for why some people earn a lot of money and others don't, not only in the City but elsewhere. It is simply a question of economics.

From the perspective of my Longest Standing Girlfriend it is easy to see why City salaries look inflated. She has worked just as hard at her career and earned just as many academic plaudits as anyone on a trading floor. She has a first degree in engineering and two masters degrees – one in marketing and an MBA from Cranfield. She worked for almost her entire career, some sixteen years, for a global drinks company head-quartered in the UK. During this time LSG lived and worked in Sydney, Scotland, Detroit and Bristol. Over time she became responsible for ever-increasing budgets, and for brands that were household names and key profit earners for her employer. Yet at the height of LSG's career, even after adding up all the benefits that she enjoyed in her employ-ment (private health cover, pensions, cars and bonuses) there would probably still have been change from £100,000 per annum.

As it happens, £100,000 per annum is probably the aver-age City salary (before benefits and bonuses) for what are termed 'front office' staff. Along with much other City vocab-ulary, this is not a literal description. Investment bank personnel may be roughly grouped into 'front' and 'back' office staff. They may of course all work in the same office and even the same room. However, front office staff are those who deal with the clients, while the back office are those who support them. Thus a salesman on the trading floor (a front office employee) undertakes a trade on behalf of a client. Once the trade has been completed, the back office will ensure that the share or bond ownership, and the cash, change hands within the appropriate time and with all the supporting paperwork.

I have heard the front office described as 'skilled' and the back office as 'unskilled'. This is a long way from the truth;

while it is true that few graduate-calibre people are put to work in the back office, it would be an erroneous generalisation to talk about the function as unskilled. Parts of the job are very complicated, and an inefficient back office can lead to fund management clients deliberately choosing not to deal with a particular investment bank. Similarly I promise you that I could find front office people in every bank for whom 'skilled' would be a laughable description.

Why is the City able to pay such salaries? Why is there such a premium for people who work there? It is quite simply that the City is able to make a large amount of what economists call 'super-normal profits'. The volumes traded across the market every day are so enormous that you need only a small fraction of a percentage of a margin to make many millions of pounds. The difference between the cost of some government debt and the sum acquired by selling it to somebody else might be very small – a typical bond spread is less than a fraction of a penny per bond traded – but multiply this by many millions and you will see why the figures start to rack up. And all this can be achieved by one man sitting at a desk with a telephone, a Reuters screen and a Herman Miller Aeron chair. Of course, he needs a lot of capital behind him, provided by the bank's shareholders, but at the end of the day the costs involved in processing this kind of money are not, compared to the rewards, that expensive. And it is very transparent how much some of these people make for their employer. Traders in particular can see exactly how much profit (or loss) they are bringing in.

Andrew Analyst is a typical equities analyst. Let's say he follows the pharmaceutical sector, and is instrumental in providing research and commentary as well as valuations on the world's top pharmaceutical companies. Let's assume he is very highly rated by the fund management industry, who regularly vote him top of the pops and give a lot of business to his company. They are anxious to get him to continue to impart his words of wisdom, and so will have to direct a reasonable amount of commission his way, or at least to his employers.

In fact, all fund managers are anxious to ensure that they get the leading analysts' bons mots. The smaller among them may find that the big investment banks set them commission targets. If enough commission is not forthcoming, they will find themselves cut off, and the analysts working for that bank will not call them, nor will they be able to access the bank's research the minute it is published. Of course, the table turns with the bigger fund managers. The last thing any investment banker wants is to be struck off the dealing list of a major fund manager, someone like Fidelity, say.

So Andrew Analyst is responsible for a lot of commission being paid to his employer by fund managers. But there will be another, much more valuable, revenue stream that the bank enjoys courtesy of Mr Analyst. He happens to work at an investment bank whose corporate finance department is an adviser to Megapharmaceutical plc. Megapharmaceutical is a monolithic organisation, stretching around the world, flogging anti-Aids and asthma drugs to everyone and making a small fortune, regularly acquiring other companies and having to be advised when this happens. Needless to say they will pay out millions in advisory fees, and no doubt Andrew's bonus will reflect this to some extent. Why should this be the case? After all, the fee is paid to corporate finance for their advice. Ah, but corporate finance couldn't do their job without Andrew. He is their key industry source of information. He also has reach and influence with the fund managers who own Megapharmaceutical's shares and who might choose to buy (or sell) them on the basis of his advice. Megapharmaceutical like having access to Andrew via the corporate finance department at the bank, and they are certainly prepared to pay for the privilege.

It is possible that Megapharmaceutical plc will still use the bank to advise them if Andrew walks across the road to Merrill Lynch – but equally possibly they might go to Merrill Lynch. If you managed this bank, wouldn't you pay Andrew as well as you could possibly afford to?

Knowing that graduates start in the City on £40,000 a year, you might think that the most senior people would be on phenomenal salaries. The truth is that most banks try to cap basic salaries at a reasonably low rate in favour of a performance-related pay element. The argument goes that if the bank doesn't perform very well the wage bill will be commensurately low. In practice, of course, this is never the case – if the bank performs very badly it won't wish to lose all its talented staff, who might, just possibly, help them perform better the following year. However, their definition of 'reasonably low' might be different to that of the average person, with front office salaries averaging around £100,000. This may sound impressive, but very few people I know in the City would bother to work there if they thought £100,000 was all they would earn that year.

Even for the brief time that I was nominally in charge of several hundred people scattered around the globe, the most expensive person on my payroll was paid a basic salary of £200,000. This, of course, would never have got him (yes, him) out of bed in the morning if he thought it was all he was going to earn.

So why do people in the City get out of bed in the morning? How do they earn the million-pound-plus annual pay-outs? Bonuses are the quick answer, and we will return to these. But there is another way in which many people in the City make a lot of money for themselves. They invest in stocks, shares, bonds and other capital market instruments with their own money, and in many cases make handsome profits. These days there are lots of rules and regulations to prevent their activity from prejudicing their ability to act on behalf of clients (see Chapter 5), but it is still possible to turn your small nest egg into a much bigger one if you are an astute reader of the markets.

When I worked on a trading floor I was for a while privileged to sit next to a man who had a legendary ability to pick which shares were going to increase in value. For this reason he was beloved of both his clients and also his colleagues, many of whom followed him blindly into every investment, convinced that he could never be wrong. As it happened, he rarely was. To this day he continues to work on a trading floor, although I am not sure why, as he must have amassed a vast personal fortune many years ago.

Some time in the early part of 1999, the bank where he was working employed a secretary who shared his surname. I doubt whether he ever met this woman, as they sat in different parts of a vast trading floor. At the end of the year she left the bank's employ after several confrontations with her manager about excess days off. And that was that, or so everyone thought.

In early 2000, the personnel department contacted our popular man and asked him whether he had changed his bank account. He replied that he had banked at exactly the same place for the entire time he had been in their employ. Why had they asked? It emerged that they had tried to pay his bonus into his bank account and it had been refused. Some eagle-eyed bank clerk, alert as they should always be to signs of money laundering, had noted an unusually large sum destined for the account, and had refused to accept it.

Our man was perplexed. His bonus that year was large, as 1999 had been a good year, but not exceptionally so. Indeed, he had received larger ones in the past. So why had his bank thought it so odd? He asked the personnel department to check again.

They returned rather red faced. It wasn't his bank account they had been trying to pay the bonus into – it was the bank account of the long-departed secretary. There was worse to come. It turned out that they had been paying his monthly salary into her account as well, ever since she had joined, some eleven months earlier. And what had they been paying into his? Er . . . nothing.

If you were not paid your monthly salary for eleven months, would you notice? I certainly would! When the police were called, as they had to be, they were immediately suspicious of our man on the trading floor. What sort of person doesn't notice that his salary has not been paid for eleven months? Surely he must have been up to no good, and had been nervous of drawing attention to himself.

The police (average salary somewhere around £35,000) had to learn what we already know about a lot of people in the City – their monthly salary is essentially just pin money. Our popular man on the trading floor had been making so much money from his personal investments in 1999, at the height of the dot.com boom, that his salary was of little significance to him. In comparison to the money he was banking from his own trading, it was small beer. No wonder he hadn't missed it.

* * *

Sadly, I never got anywhere near the millions of pounds that some of my peers pocketed. While admittedly earning slightly more than the average man on the street, I never made it into the mega league. You might ask why, and the answer is quite simple – I was a woman. Aha, I hear you cry, that old chestnut about women being discriminated against in the City.

It is not as simple as saying if you're a woman you are paid badly and if you are a man you are paid well. The real truth is that if you are a woman working in the City you are very unlikely to change jobs as often as a man. I have never seen any statistics on this, and therefore can't prove it, but I promise you that women change jobs far less often. They are more loyal, more nurturing, they appreciate the strength of the internal networks they build up inside the organisations they work for, and they are not prepared to flit from place to place every eighteen months in search of the next guaranteed bonus. As a direct result of this, the banks that employ them can afford to pay them less because they are very unlikely to move. What more than anything else in the City guarantees that you are well paid is the threat that you might leave. The combination of the fact that women are less likely to move and the fact that disloyalty is so highly rewarded has made women lose out, particularly at bonus time. Look at all these compensation cases that have been in the newspapers over the last couple of years – Julie Bower, Louise Barton, etc. At the end of the day they were all about bonuses, not salaries. (It is worth noting, by the way, that Louise Barton had worked at the same place for sixteen years.)

So how do you get better paid as a woman? Be more visible (think Nicola Horlick, Robin Saunders). Move job more often. Be more productive. All these things require such an enormous amount of effort and energy and, more to the point, time, that you may prefer to survive as I did, simply by being content with being better paid than the man in the street rather than benchmarking yourself against the highest-paid people in the business. Greed and envy are never attractive traits, and especially not in a woman.

Bonuses, of course, are a ridiculous feature of the City of London. The typical bonus process is as subjective as it is possible to be. Every year the senior managers of the average investment bank will be contacted and asked for their estimates of what bonuses should be allocated to each of their staff. As a manager, I would dutifully send off the requested information by the appointed date, having of course sought the input of my team leaders (head of sales, head of research, and so forth). The figures would be returned from head office after about three weeks with a request to cut them by anything up to 50 per cent. Having been down this road before, I had of course submitted figures that were massively inflated in the first place. Now down to more realistic figures, I sent them off again. A week or so later back they came again with another request to cut them, this time by 25–40 per cent.

Now I would really be getting into trouble. What on earth was I going to do? The first thing, of course, is to look at the list and work out who might leave if you don't pay them more money. The whole thing is the most extraordinarily subjective exercise. In fact, bonuses are the only instance I know where it is possible to hand millions of pounds out to a group of people and be absolutely sure of one thing – they will all be unhappy. I handed out bonuses for my last three years at the bank and I hated every single minute of it.

I became a stockbroker in September 1992 and my first bonus cheque was handed to me in March 1993. It was based on a calendar year, so clearly I only qualified for three and a half months' credit. I went in to see the head of research, who pushed an envelope across the table to me. 'Here you are,' he said. 'As my father used to say when he handed over my pocket money, don't spend it all on LPs.' I left the room and opened the envelope. My gross bonus was about £1,200, a little under £800 net. I was 30 years old and this was not a very large sum of money. However, times were tough in 1992 and I suppose I was lucky to get anything at all. This set the tone for the next few years. Because I was moved around the world so much, and in and out of different profit centres, people always disowned me when it came to bonus time. I got wise to this towards the end of my City career, and every time I was asked to move I demanded money up front from the unit that wished to employ me. The internal transfer market is not dead, and I managed to get a signing-on bonus (see below) at least twice from different departments as I moved around the bank.

My second year was worse. I had managed to persuade the bank to pay off my outstanding fees at the London Business School, some £7,500. To them this was an eminently suitable arrangement. It was completely tax deductible and didn't attract employer's national insurance. (There's another good story. It used to be the case that if you paid bonuses in anything other than cash you didn't have to pay this tax, which the Chancellor has recently increased. Hence for a period of time bonuses were handed out in gold bars, shares and virtually anything that was easily convertible into cash without actually being cash at the time of the donation.) This particular year the bank had dreadful cash flow problems and so the bonuses were divided into two parts, one paid early in the year and the other in September. This also had the effect of preventing people leaving the day after their bonuses were paid, a practice that still tends to go on today. We were all kept back after work. By now the market had closed and effectively we could be given our bonuses in shares (yet another trick that at the time could be used to avoid employer's National Insurance). Having waited with great anticipation for an hour, I was called at my desk by the head of personnel. 'Mrs M, I just wanted to tell you that you won't be called in to be given a bonus. Your bonus for the year is going to be £15,000, and as it is payable in two halves, and you have to pay us back half for your school fees, you won't be seeing a penny today.'

I was absolutely devastated. To be fair, the man had magnanimously said that if this posed cash flow problems for me they would be happy to advance me some money against the September payment, but this was hardly the same thing. But I didn't have time to get seriously miserable – things were hotting up in the meeting room next door.

In those days I sat on a trading desk row of four. One of the three other people was a highly volatile Italian. He had been summoned in by the head of sales to be given his bonus cheque, and what I could hear through the prefabricated wall that separated us certainly helped distract me from my own misery at having no extra cash to go home with that night. The derision with which this particular individual greeted the sum of money that he was being given cannot be exaggerated. His comments went something like this: 'Call this a bonus? It is more like a tip! I am not an Italian waiter! I think this is an insult! I will donate it to charity! No, on second thoughts this is far too insulting a sum to give to any charity. It is so low, I leave it for you to spend as you wish. I am completely horrified.' At this point the door slammed open and the individual stormed across the room and out of the building, never to be seen again.

Many years later I wrote about this in my weekly column, then in the weekend *FT*. I rarely named names in my column, and was rather startled to receive, within twenty-four hours, an e-mail from this Italian, someone I hadn't spoken to or heard of for seven years. 'Dear Mrs M,' it said, 'you may like to know that after my exit I went to serve the coffee and pizza in a little outfit around the corner called Collins Stewart.' Collins Stewart was, in early 1994 when he joined, a small stockbroker, comprising less than sixteen people. It has since got much bigger, much more profitable, and is a listed company in its own right on the London Stock Exchange, capitalised at over £600 million. I suspect he may have made a lot more money by moving there than he ever would have done had he remained that day.

His choice of Collins Stewart amused me as it is run by one of the most combustible individuals I have ever met. The thought of the Italian and him working together in what was then a relatively small operation was mind-boggling. How they have managed to remain on reasonable terms all this time without thumping each other or screaming obscenities I have no idea. Presumably his new boss finds his cheque book a little easier to open when it comes to bonus time.

* * *

One of the most tricky situations I faced personally was in Japan, when an analyst complained that his bonus was smaller than his wife's. I explained that his wife worked in a completely different bank and I had absolutely no control over what she was or wasn't paid. He was being paid for his performance and what he was being paid was in line with what other people within our own organisation were receiving. What had his wife got to do with it? I was then informed it was a very important matter of personal face and that I had probably destroyed his marriage by not paying him more than his wife.

I tell this story to show how far removed from performance bonuses have become. The tribunal hearing in the Louise Barton case made a decision based in part on their industrial knowledge that 'it is a vital component of the City bonus culture that bonuses are discretionary, scheme rules are unwritten and individual bonuses are not revealed'. At the time this book went to press, Louise Barton was appealing against the decision of the original tribunal, funded by the Equal Opportunities Commission, which had also supported the eventually victorious Julie Bower. Julie Mellor, the EOC chair, has argued that the way in which pay and bonuses are decided needs to be transparent throughout the labour market and the City 'cannot be regarded as a special case'.

I would support this in part and reject it in part. It is certainly true that bonuses should be less dependent on who has a gun to your head and rather should be based on how people genuinely contributed to the company's performance over the previous twelve months. But they can never be formula-driven. The City is now so complex a place that no one person can generate income single-handedly. Today's stockbroker may well talk regularly to a fund manager and feed them all manner of useful investment ideas. The fund manager will then, in appreciation, direct commission to that broker. But it may not be in a way that will get the individual broker rewarded – I have frequently given a client a brilliant Japanese investment idea only to be rewarded with a massive order in the shares of a Swedish company. This will naturally be credited to my Swedish colleagues. Rewarding my Swedish colleagues for this order in the form of higher bonuses is as appropriate as finding out what people's wives are paid and matching their compensation accordingly.

* * *

While on the subject of bonuses, I was once told a story about someone who was running the recently acquired stock-broking division of a particular bank. This man had been a partner in the firm which had been sold to the bank, and was a firm believer in the City motto 'My word is my bond'. It was a difficult year, and in order to maintain the loyalty of the team he had recruited around him he promised a small number of key individuals guaranteed bonuses of approximately £100,000 each. At the end of the year the parent bank informed this chap that there would be little or no money available for distribution in his division. 'But what about the people I have promised these bonuses to?' he asked. 'Well, we didn't promise them, you did, so you will just have to explain that they won't be forthcoming,' came the answer.

The chap was completely incensed by this and made the decision to leave the bank, never to darken its doors again. But before he did, his last gesture was to get out his personal cheque book and write cheques to the individuals concerned, for £100,000 each. As you can imagine, these people would now follow this man to the ends of the earth.

* * *

One of the ways in which changing jobs can actually increase your income is by virtue of the signing-on bonus. Quite simply, this is a sum of money handed over in return for your signing a contract agreeing to work somewhere, hence its name. Guaranteed bonuses can also help to increase your income. As I have said, most investment banks work to the calendar year, and therefore bonuses are paid out in the spring of the following year. Anybody resigning after their bonus who is on a reasonable amount of notice (many senior people are on six months' or a year's notice, a subject we will return to shortly) couldn't hope to start at any rival establishment much before June or July at the earliest. Knowing that they are likely to serve not even half a year with their new employer, they will insist on a guaranteed bonus at the end of that year, to make sure they are not discriminated against.

The real killer about guaranteed bonuses, as John Mack found recently at CSFB, is how unfair they are to incumbent staff. If your bonus pool is fixed and most of it is accounted-for guarantees, then the people who have worked for you for a while and served loyally, and who are often key to your operation, have to be fed from the scraps that remain after the guarantees are handed out.

But let's consider the case of a mythical investment bank, which, let's say, desperately needs a pharmaceutical analyst. It is already October. They approach Andrew Analyst, but he is not having any of it. It has been a good year for his employer and he knows that his bonus is assured. He is so close to the end of the financial year that it is very unlikely that anything will go wrong. He has no intention of moving.

So what are they to do? Andrew is the man they want. The answer is to ask what his bonus will be the following March and offer it to him immediately on joining, thereby getting him to resign immediately (or at least after a protracted negotiation over pay and rations), probably about the beginning of November.

Anyone who resigns at the beginning of November has either got a whacking great sign-on bonus where they are going or is a complete dodo and has no expectations of cash in the spring. In our example, of course, Andrew Analyst has been asked what he thinks his bonus will be the following spring and will have doubled it. This sum will then be paid to him the day he starts work for his new employer. In addition, he will have made absolutely sure that he is going to get a guaranteed bonus at the end of the year.

Now we come to the issue of notice. Let's say that our Andrew is on six months' notice. His current employer has three choices. They can continue to let him come to work, research the top pharmaceutical companies, speak to their fund management client base, advise their corporate clients and build his relationship with both sets of clients, all in preparation for the day he moves to the rival. This clearly would be commercial suicide. Or they can let him off his notice period, and allow him to join his new employer as soon as he wishes. In the United States this is very common, but in the United Kingdom it is highly unlikely that any investment banker would let a top-rated analyst move to his or her new employer before the end of their notice period.

More usually, a third strategy is employed. Andrew's employers will continue to pay him for the six months of his notice and have him sit 'out of the market' in order to prevent the new employer from gaining an advantage. And so, on the day of his resignation, Andrew Analyst will be sent home, his security pass cancelled, his car-parking space eagerly eyed up by other people in the building. He will then remain at home (or on an exotic holiday) for the duration of his notice period, even if it is six months. During this time he will be paid every month as normal and will use the time to go hunting, shooting, fishing, skiing or whatever it is that particularly grabs him.

This experience of being at home, unable to join a new employer but also unable to continue to work for an existing one, is known in the trade as gardening leave. Presumably this is because people originally used to spend this time peacefully in their gardens. Now that most highly paid City analysts are under 35 and live in penthouse flats in Spitalfields, I presume they are using the time for other things. Being paid to be on holiday full-time for six months sounds like everyone's dream. It certainly would be mine.

While Andrew Analyst is being pursued by his new employer, he is in a very strong position. He will be able to make sure that his first year's bonus will not be compromised in any way, and if he is sensible his second year's as well. He will therefore negotiate with his new employer a two-year guaranteed arrangement, whereby his bonus will be guaranteed not to fall below a minimum threshold.

Loyalty is almost unfailingly unrewarding in the City. The only way to get a guaranteed bonus while remaining *in situ* is to pursue an alternative job somewhere else, then resign and allow yourself to be bought back by getting your current employer to match the offer you have received from outside, including the guaranteed bonus. Grossly unfair? Show me any industry in the Western world that is consistently fair. The City is no different from anywhere else.

* * *

What do people spend all this money on? Houses, for a start. They buy second homes (in the country, for weekends) and then holiday houses (in France, for example) and then, when they have enough of these (winter and summer), they move on to yachts. Yachts fit in well with another area where money is thrown around by people in the City – sport and leisure interests. People in the City earning huge sums of money are more likely than anyone else to shoot, fish and jump horses over fences (or own horses that jump over fences – or even run in a straight line).

Another favoured way of redistributing all this income is via luxury car dealers. I was told of a trader who went home late one Friday night much the worse for wear. Catching his usual train to somewhere in deepest Essex, he knew better than to drive his luxury car home at the end of the journey. He instead summoned a taxi company to supply a driver to take the wheel. Once home, while waiting for the company to collect their driver, the trader made an additional request. Would the driver mind returning to the station car park and bringing back one at a time the three remaining cars the trader had parked there?

School fees are another drain down which money is poured from the City. Large families, all educated privately, are still the preserve of the wealthy. I have met more people working in the City with three or more children than anywhere else – even Ireland. When, in 2002, the so-called 'split capital' scandal broke, concerning people allegedly being mis-sold investments that turned out to substantially decline in value, seasoned observers commented that the hue and cry over the affair was simply due to the fact that such schemes had been much used as an investment for school fees, and nothing upsets middle England more than not being able to educate its children privately. (Incidentally, more capital had been destroyed in the same period, as some-one pointed out to me, from the collapse in the share price of

3i, but no one was establishing a House of Commons select committee to investigate that.)

Finally, women and sex can get pretty expensive. For people in existing relationships, these have to be maintained, and apologies made for all that late-night working. For those breaking off relationships, this isn't cheap either – changing wives (or husbands) is a little easier if you earn a whole lot of money. There are also plenty of establishments in London and elsewhere ready and willing to relieve City employees of their wage packet in return for sexual entertainment, if not satisfaction – see the chapter on sex in the City.

So many other industries suffer when the City suffers. The housing market, the luxury car market, the private education market, the bespoke jewellery market – these are all more efficient at redistributing the City's wealth than Karl Marx could ever have dreamed of. There are, of course, many philanthropists around. But the City's approach to philanthropy is best summed up in the old saying: 'The best way to help the poor is not to become one of them.'

* * *

How, then, to get paid lots of money in the City, even in these days of the longest bear market in living memory? Be good at what you do (or at least sought after) and then make sure that you change jobs a lot and hold your employer to ransom. If this doesn't sit easily with you, then learn to be content with 'normal' rates of pay, as I was. When I started in the City it was on a basic salary of £35k. I left on a basic salary of £110k. My bonuses were invariably nothing to write home about as I lost out to people who held a gun to the head of our managers. But I was happy, and I loved my job.

And I am not alone. As this book was going to press I went to a big City dinner at a swanky Mayfair hotel, and ran into the man who wasn't paid for eleven months, the man who has for many years been famous for identifying shares that are likely to increase in value. Why, I asked him, was he still working? He didn't need the money, bonuses were thin if not non-existent, he has no children to provide for. 'Mrs M,' he said, 'I love working in the City. There is nothing else I would rather be doing.'

Chapter 5

Big Brother is Watching

Big Brother is Watching

THE CITY IS HEAVILY POLICED these days, and I am not talking about the bobby on the beat. No, the real policemen are to found outside the Square Mile, down in a towering office in Canary Wharf. The Financial Services Authority (FSA) is the all-encompassing regulatory body conceived and established by the Labour government that came to power in 1997. It is a non-governmental body, and was given its statutory powers by the Financial Services and Markets Act 2000.

It employs two thousand people who toil to try to ensure that all aspects of the financial services industry constitute a level playing field.

It was not always thus. As recently as twenty years ago, the City was almost completely self-regulated. Why has it become necessary to mount such a vast and monolithic operation to keep it under control?

The argument for a level playing field is based on the view that unequal access to information will cause markets to function imperfectly, and thus liquidity will dry up. For example, say you are thinking of buying shares in Sainsbury's. But what if other, bigger, investors have more up-to-date trading information unavailable to you? You might be just about to buy shares the day before Sainsbury's issue a profit warning. You don't know that the profit warning is forthcoming, but perhaps a few brokers and fund managers receive advance notice. So they sell shares while you, the complete mug, go ahead and buy them.

That would patently be unfair, and if you really thought that Sainsbury's, if they were about to issue a profit warning, went around telling a few favoured people in advance you'd probably not bother to trade at all. And if others followed your example, so the volume of shares traded – the liquidity – would dry up.

Of course, it is illegal for Sainsbury's to tell a few people that they are going to issue a profit warning. They have to make a public statement and tell everyone at the same time. Clearly, there will be a few people inside the company who *will* know in advance – the finance director, for instance – but it is illegal for him to tell other people and also to sell shares he owns personally before the information is public. And if his wife looks over his shoulder while he is drafting the press release in bed, it is illegal for her to sell or buy shares until the information is in the public domain.

You have to understand that the City, and indeed the government, is inordinately proud of the fact that, despite being located on a small, obscure island off the coast of France with pretty horrible weather and a mediocre-sized economy, London remains one of the key financial centres in the world. Anything that might jeopardise this is taken very seriously, and anything that might make people choose to transact business somewhere else is stamped on without mercy.

As I mentioned, up until 1979 the City was almost completely self-regulating. The Prevention of Fraud (Investments) Act 1959 existed to deal with serious white-collar crime, but there was nothing to tackle those involved in insider dealing, which in its present form was not made illegal until the 1980s. The Banking Act (1979) was the first effort to regulate the City and allowed the Bank of England to regulate other banks.

The reason behind the increase in regulation at the start of the 1980s was that, owing to increased privatisation and the idea of a 'share-owning democracy', it appeared grossly unfair not to provide protection for the public from what were perceived to be the sharper City practices, such as dealing on information received before the public got hold of it. Allowing the continuation of insider dealing would have resulted in market liquidity drying up.

The next key bit of legislation was the Financial Services Act 1986, which created a number of 'membership-based' regulatory bodies, controlling stockbroking, retail financial services, fund management, and so on. Every investment bank, fund management company and other financial services firm was required to belong to its industry association, and they were collectively regulated by the Securities and Investments Board (SIB). The FSA has effectively replaced this plethora of organisations.

The Takeover Panel is essentially the one remaining self-regulatory body in the City of London and has no legal powers whatsoever. It exists to watch out for cowboy behaviour on the part of companies taking over other companies. Breaches of its code are punished not by fines but effectively by excluding the banks and brokers involved in the transaction. It's as though they are saying 'play by our rules or we won't play with you at all'. It is funded by its members and staffed by people on secondment from those members. Cynics suggest that as these people are only in their posts temporarily and will return to their employer after a couple of years, they are unlikely to deal harshly with member firms found to have broken the code. Be that as it may, the Takeover Panel continues in force and nothing statutory has been proposed to take its place.

The Takeover Panel can claim credit for calling for insider dealing to be made an offence, having realised that their code was not stringent enough. Thus it was that the Companies Act 1980 was the first piece of legislation to criminalise insider dealing. Subsequently, two other important pieces of legislation were enacted – the Criminal Justice Act 1987 and the Criminal Justice Act 1993.

The Criminal Justice Act 1987 established the Serious Fraud Office (SFO) under the auspices of the Attorney General. The SFO is both investigator and prosecutor, directed by senior lawyers and accountants, and borrows police detectives from the Met and other forces. Its extensive powers (those under investigation have no right to silence) have been heavily criticised by the European Court of Human Rights, especially in relation to the prosecution of Ernest Saunders for his role in the Guinness scandal, originally uncovered in 1986. For those of you too young or without long enough memories to recall this, Saunders was found to have employed every trick in the book to prop up the price of the company he ran, Guinness, while it was trying to acquire another company, Distillers. The reason he did this was because Guinness had offered to buy Distillers shares in exchange for Guinness shares – clearly the higher the Guinness share price, the more attractive the offer and the more likely it was to succeed.

You can look on Ernest Saunders as a crook, because he broke several laws, primarily contravening a number of Companies Acts. The alternative is to see him as a driven man determined to achieve the best possible results for his shareholders. Either way, he was investigated by the Department of Trade and Industry (DTI) and then the SFO, and, in contrast to the situation in a normal police investigation, he was compelled to answer their inspectors' questions, since, as mentioned, the SFO can insist on this.

Saunders's case is a good example of how the creeping hand of regulation in the City has extended as far as Strasbourg – the European Court of Human Rights did not rule against the verdict (it could have done), but it was deemed that his trial had been unfair because he had been compelled to answer questions.

The SFO can't instigate its own investigations, but is referred cases by the DTI, police forces or any other official body. It now deals with the vast majority of criminal offences involving massive fraud or theft. These should be distinguished from 'market abuse' cases, which fall under the jurisdiction of the FSA and are civil as opposed to criminal. Misdemeanours dealt with by the FSA are supposedly technical breaches, which often occur through sloppiness with no ill intent. It also deals with the mistreatment of consumers, which can straddle the border between a criminal and a civil offence. As can be imagined, there is quite a lot of friction between the SFO and the FSA, and the former is adamantly opposed to the latter having any criminal prosecution role.

Between 1988 and 1991 the SFO was a great hit with the press. The arrest of Asil Nadir for his involvement in the Polly Peck scandal was highly commended in the pages of national papers. Likewise, the arrests of Kevin and Ian

Maxwell after the collapse of their father's media empire received rapturous applause. It became less popular as cases started to go wrong in court. Ernest Saunders had his sentence cut by half on appeal. Blue Arrow, a case in which the market in shares of an employment agency was rigged, resulted in the prosecution of fourteen individual and corporate defendants, but subsequently fell apart.

The Serious Fraud Office still exists today, as an independent government department that investigates and prosecutes serious or complex fraud. It is part of the UK criminal justice system, although it has no powers of jurisdiction in Scotland, the Isle of Man or the Channel Islands. Revolutionary in its day, when little regulation existed in the City and criminal prosecutions were almost unheard of, it is now part of a far wider regulatory infrastructure that is dominated by the FSA, no longer known to the public in the same way for its headline-grabbing escapades.

* * *

My own experience of regulation was (thank goodness) a long way from that of Asil Nadir and Ernest Saunders. The only real evidence of regulation (known in the City as 'compliance') that I encountered in my early years in the Square Mile was the fact that all our telephone conversations were tape-recorded. This only seemed to apply to the trading positions, rather than the research department or the back office, but even so, for several hundred people every single day, every time they picked up the telephone the tape recorder was switched on. At least, that was the theory. In practice, the tape recorders broke down and all the usual problems that bedevil information technology, even in the early nineties, cropped up. By the time the eighties had turned into the nineties, every stockbroker had its own compliance officer, initially seen as a job for someone who wasn't yet prepared to accept retirement but had largely outlived their usefulness elsewhere in the company. Today this has all changed. Rottweiler-like lawyers are much in evidence in the City, earning piles of money to oversee compliance. The City is running scared of its regulators and anxious to avoid huge fines and unnecessary publicity for non-compliance.

My own boss, the elder of the Arrogant Twosome, used to dread listening to tapes. I vividly recall flying back to the office from an overseas assignment to find him looking supremely glum as he headed off upstairs to the compliance officer's department. One of the salespeople had come into possession of reasonably sensitive information about a company's accounts through a chum working in the finance department there. He decided unwisely to use the information to show off to a fund management client, but he picked the wrong guy to telephone. Not only did the fund manager terminate the call but he did the correct thing and placed the company's shares on the restricted stock list. Every bank and fund management institution has such a list, the composition of which varies daily. It is a central list of company shares that cannot be traded by anyone in the organisation because either someone somewhere in the organisation is aware of sensitive information, as in this case, or they are acting on behalf of the company concerned or a company that is planning a bid for it.

The fund management client was very cross, especially as his organisation held a large position in the company's shares and now they would be unable to buy or sell them until after the next set of financial results had been published. He immediately telephoned our head of equity sales and complained that the salesman had made him, the client, an insider. The tapes were summoned. The real problem was that this particular salesperson had an unbelievably boring line of patter. There was no way of knowing at what point in the tape the conversation with this client had occurred and the information had been divulged. So there was nothing for it but to sit and listen to nearly one and a half hours of this person's dreary conversation. Some of it was so mind-numbingly embarrassing and awful that my boss and the compliance officer sat with their heads in their hands, listening to the salesperson make inane jokes, indulge in base banter and even talk about interesting subjects in an incredibly dull fashion. What a way to make a living!

* * *

After taped conversations, the next sign that the long hand of regulation was stealthily moving across the City was when changes were introduced to the way in which banks entertained their fund management clients. As I have explained, it is absolutely paramount as a stockbroker to build strong and lasting relationships with the fund managers to whom you speak daily. They are your number one priority, and no time and effort can be spared in developing their positive views of your bank and its employees. In my own first job in the City, as a specialist salesperson, it was imperative that I persuade as many fund managers as possible of the merits of the Arrogant Twosome.

To this end I was positively encouraged to entertain fund managers and their staff at every opportunity. I took them to the opera, the theatre, polo matches and even to the pub. I recall some of our most successful fund manager entertainment evenings involved renting a room in a nearby hostelry when a major football match was being televised. We even targeted lady fund manager clients by persuading very upmarket shops in seriously swanky locations to open their doors in the evening in the run-up to Christmas, and laying on champagne and a unique shopping opportunity plus a small gift for everyone as they left. Tying up these promotional evenings with luxury goods manufacturers took up masses of time, and was another skill that I never learnt at business school.

For one of my more memorable client lunches I hired a stretch limousine, put a bottle of champagne and three glasses in the back, and whipped around the corner to take a senior fund manager and one of his department out to lunch at La Tante Claire, a restaurant in Chelsea, a long way from the City. It was a jolly good lunch and a very entertaining journey both there and back, sitting behind the dark windows peering out at people looking at this extraordinary vehicle, then rarely seen in the City of London. I was rather proud of myself for having had such an original idea.

This was nothing, though. One bank used to take all their fixed-income fund manager clients off to Switzerland for a few days' skiing each year. Similarly, if a public company wished to apprise fund managers of the merits of investing in it, it would lay on luxurious foreign trips. I remember, as a young girl working in financial PR, being involved when Allied Lyons arranged to take a group of fund managers and analysts to see the assets of a company it was busy acquiring in Canada. Time was at a premium and we needed to get everyone there and back as quickly as we could – so we chartered Concorde.

Even without Concorde, being a fund manager could be the passport to any number of luxurious travel opportunities in the early 1990s. Going off to view the latest foreign acquisition was absolutely par for the course, whether it was a week spent in Latin America, a visit to a spectacular hotel and golf course on the west coast of the United States, or a trip to Australia to look at a gold mine. The tab would be picked up by the company itself or by the investment bank that had advised it. Anything to win over those fund managers!

At some point the City decided that enough was enough. The word was gently put out to fund managers that perhaps it was a conflict of interest to accept quite so much hospitality from companies wishing to promote investment in their shares. Eventually, any fund manager wishing to accept hospitality or a gift from either a broker or a public company, over a set value (normally a nominal £10 or so), would have to clear it with their own compliance officers. This put paid to the skiing pretty quickly! It would probably have put paid to the stretch limousine as well, if I had ever told my clients exactly how much it had cost.

The next step on the regulatory road was the introduction of restrictions on buying and selling stocks and shares for oneself. Known in the City as trading on one's personal account, or 'trading PA', this was highlighted briefly in the chapter on pay as one of the main ways (other than through salaries and bonuses) by which people in the City amass substantial personal wealth.

For most people in the City who have been there for any length of time, personal account trading is the only game in town. What is the point of working for an organisation that gives you unlimited real-time access to information as it breaks if you are not able to use that information for personal gain? Over the years, many people I worked with would expect to make as much money from trading their own personal portfolios as they would working on behalf of the bank or its clients. And for many years, anything went. If you received a particularly hot tip about a stock, of course you called your clients and told them about it, but not before you placed your own order. Many people still around in the City built fortunes on what is now known as insider trading. Prior to 1980, rather than being considered a crime, it was regarded as clever to have information ahead of everyone else. However, through the eighties, and even more in the nineties, the long hand of regulation began to encroach over this practice too. I know many people who worked on years after they could have retired because the trading floor gave them access to screens and information vital to maintaining their own investments. Once the regulations started to make PA trading tougher, they all retired.

The only requirement regarding personal dealing when I first joined my employer in September 1992 was that if we wished to deal on our own personal account we had to open an account with a stockbroker designated by the bank. This was because we as an organisation didn't deal with individuals, focused as we were on the needs of large institutional fund managers. (Brokers that deal with individual investors are known as private client brokers, and largely service the needs of wealthy individuals.)

Every time I rang my broker to undertake a transaction, a copy of the dealing advice slip would be sent to my head of compliance. I have no idea what he did with these slips; he certainly never came to ask me about them. I remember vividly buying and selling Capital Radio shares a total of five times in four weeks during 1993, in a successful attempt to make enough money to pay the next three terms' worth of private nursery fees for son number one. I didn't have any inside information on Capital Radio; it was just that the shares kept on going up and I kept taking profits and then deciding to get back in again. By the time I came back to work in England in 1996 after a stint overseas, things had moved on a bit. Now if I wanted to buy company shares for my own personal portfolio I had to seek prior permission if the company was in an industry sector that I followed. However, for all other investments I was able to go ahead and do exactly what I wished.

These days it is all very different. Compliance reaches right down the line. If you want to deal you submit a form, often (in the most modern establishments) electronically, detailing what you wish to buy or sell. A computer automatically checks your request against a restricted stock list, and by return e-mail grants or denies you permission. Then and only then may you proceed. You may also have absolutely no holdings in companies that you personally follow as an analyst, and you are only allowed to dispose of your PA holdings at certain times of the year.

Now that PA dealing has become so troublesome, many people do not bother. My Most Socially Acceptable Girlfriend, a PA investor through and through, continues to persevere. MSAG was one of the original trust fund girls, and so trades in rather larger quantities than the average person of her age and income. Permission to trade requires her to fill in a form manually and get it signed by her Chief Investment Officer.

Therein lies the first hurdle, psychological though it may be. MSAG's employer is not a large organisation, although it manages billions of pounds. Thus she knows her CIO quite well. Information on what investments you are making is akin to information on your sex life – i.e. it is probably something you would rather keep to yourself. Writing out a list of what you are buying and selling and when and handing it to someone else is giving away more than most people, and certainly MSAG, would prefer to do.

Of course, the CIO is usually out or in a meeting when she goes to his office with her dealing permission slip and she has to hand it to his secretary. Despite pleading with said secretary, MSAG frequently finds the dealing permission form signed and returned on her desk – face up. Like many thousands of people in the City, MSAG works in a trading-room configuration, and so now not only does the CIO and his secretary know exactly what she is up to, but so do her colleagues. The City is not a place for secrets.

MSAG should be grateful that she can get the form signed and returned in a timely fashion. The problem with manual requests to deal is that the CIO might be out for a long lunch or even away for the rest of the day, and by the time the form is returned the trading opportunity has passed. Permission is only valid for a limited period of time, say forty-eight hours, so if you want to trade thereafter you have to start all over again.

Finally, MSAG also has to request permission to trade for anyone else whose investments she is deemed to have control over – such as those of her husband. Fortunately (or not) for MSAG, her husband usually prefers to risk his money visiting the bookmaker rather than the stockbroker, but now and again he thinks a company is worth investing in. In theory he is then supposed to ask his wife to go through the whole rigmarole of filling out a dealing permission form and getting it signed before he proceeds. As MSAG says, whoever thinks that wives have control over their husband's investments has no idea how marriages work. Even if her husband could be persuaded to cede to his wife's directions regarding his personal portfolio, the chances are that she would be away visiting a company, out at lunch or whatever at the apposite time, and he would be unable to trade in any case. Not a terribly practical or realistic way of controlling personal investment.

Marriage offers endless possibilities for misinterpretation of the rules. While working in the bank I had to bid farewell to a main board director of whom I was extremely fond. His wife had bought shares in a company that the bank were well on the way to planning a bid for, just days before it was announced. This was a deal that he was known to have discussed with his fellow directors on the telephone from home. Had she or had she not known of the bid when she bought the shares? Regardless of the answer, it didn't look very good, and he had to resign not only from his job but also from the board of his country's stock exchange.

* * *

At the time I left the City, my compliance officer was a ferocious leggy blonde. For a few months I had the office next door to her, although I never seemed to come to her attention – probably a good thing!

The bank's dress code then was that, with the exception of people using the third floor – the meeting-room floor – we were all allowed to come to the office in 'smart casual' dress. This for men means no tie, a pair of chinos, a Ralph Lauren shirt and a blazer. For women it is a complete nightmare. What the hell is 'smart casual'? I either have clothes for work (suits, dresses) or clothes for home (jeans, jumpers) – 'smart casual' requires a whole new wardrobe. I never bothered.

One solution to this third-floor requirement was for people to bring in more formal clothes and change into them if they had a meeting. I started to notice that my compliance officer had a couple of suits hanging up in her office. Then she had another couple, and another, plus a collection of very smart shoes. I surmised that compliance was getting pretty busy – maybe masses of meetings on the third floor with the SFO? By the time her whole office resembled a wardrobe I had decided to ask her what was going on, and whether I should expect us to be closed down any day by the regulatory authorities. It turned out to be nothing of the sort – she was planning to leave her husband, and in advance of actually doing so had been spiriting away her wardrobe in order not to have to hire an articulated lorry for the final exit.

How to survive, then, in the City of 1,001 rules and regulations? There are ways and means of making life easier, although I am certainly not one to advocate criminal activity. Take the telephone taping. Why do you think there are still such a lot of payphones in the City? You might think that in this day and age of mobile telephones they would have been rendered unnecessary. However, if your office telephone is taped, and you want to make a personal call, what do you do? Your mobile phone is either paid for by your employer, in which case they see the itemised bill, or yourself, in which case your wife probably sees the bill. Ringing your mistress might be unwise. More marriages in the City (as elsewhere) have fallen apart through the unwise use of mobile telephones than for any other reason. A call to a headhunter is also something you would rather keep to yourself, and if you are in advanced negotiations with another bank over a job move it might be wise to have conversations with them from a telephone that cannot be monitored by everyone. Until they install closed-circuit TV cameras focused on the telephone boxes in Liverpool Street and Bank stations, there will always be a use for them.

PA dealing is another matter. If you don't want to be bound by the rules and regulations of your employer, then move your money to investments that don't require you to get permission to deal. Commercial property might be a good bet – no one at the FSA will be worried about your acquisition of a line of lock-up garages in Fulham. If you are one of the few people who know how to make owning racehorses a profitable business, why not try that instead? However, if you are still gripped by company shares as an investment opportunity, then try spread-betting with the likes of IG Index. Here you are essentially betting on movements in share prices rather than acquiring part ownership of companies.

Even this can get you into trouble. Paul Davidson, an entrepreneur known as 'the Plumber', recently bet that the price of a company's shares would go up after it was listed. The company was one in which he held a substantial stake. The bet was so large (£5 million) that the betting company covered its position by buying shares in the company at flotation, thus helping to ensure the success of the transaction. The FSA have been reviewing the situation and in early 2003 announced that they intend to include spread-betting within their remit, meaning that directors of companies who bet on their own shares in the run-up to the release of price-sensitive information (yes, as of today this is still legal in the UK) can be fined.

Entertaining remains the one area where self-regulation continues. Yet even here you can survive in the City and continue to be invited to smart restaurants, operas, the Chelsea Flower Show (the place to meet anyone who is anyone in the City) and major sporting events. My Most Socially Acceptable Girlfriend continues to be hosted at rugby internationals that Mr M would love to attend. One way round the rules is to entertain PA – i.e. to pay for it yourself. This may seem ludicrous – why waste your own money on entertaining your employer's clients? – but if you stand to gain personally from pulling in a big deal or becoming the highest-ranked analyst in your sector, why not throw a few lavish dinner parties or share your Arsenal season ticket? At the top end of the scale people in the City entertain PA on their yachts, in their Swiss apartments during the skiing season, and in their houses in Antigua. Relationship building is what it is all about, and a few rules and regulations are not going to impede that.

Chapter 6

Women in the City

Women in the City

THE TRUTH IS THAT THERE AREN'T that many women in the City, simply because not very many enter in the first place. On the Continent more women embark on careers in financial services. I once asked my head of human resources how come there weren't more women at more senior levels in the bank. He pointed out that, although on the Continent banks deliberately took on 50 per cent female graduate trainees, many of them fell by the wayside five years later. Training programmes in a global bank often involve overseas postings, and certainly any organisation with international pretensions would post able young people overseas at some stage. He went on to say that young single women are usually happy to take one overseas posting, but by the time it comes to the second they would rather stay at home, settle down and find somebody to marry. While I was slightly appalled by his stereotyping, I realised that he did have a point. Women are more caring individuals, less likely to abandon home, family and some semblance of a settled life in pursuit of financial gain. I don't think it is that they are any less ambitious than men; it is that they are ambitious for different things.

When the House of Commons recently debated the proposed changes to their working hours, it was argued that the reforms would make life easier for MPs, especially those women with children who are now forming an increasing proportion of Parliament. Gwyneth Dunwoody, the MP who chairs the Transport Select Committee, was incandescent with rage. She said that if women couldn't hack the hours, they shouldn't be MPs. That rather sums up my view of women in the City. If you can't hack it, don't whinge – do something else.

I am sure that most people outside think that women in the City are incredibly hard done by – certainly from reading the press you would think so. Every time a woman working for an investment bank takes her employer to an industrial tribunal for one reason or another, the case hits the headlines. Time after time we read of women who appear to have been unfairly treated, and who believe that they have been paid much worse than they would have been if they had been male.

I have to say that I don't really believe that women are paid worse than men. The real issue is that women are not prepared to behave in the same way as men do in the City.

As I have said before, the fact is that the City does not reward loyalty. If you want to be paid a lot of money, you have to move around. By resigning and moving to a different investment bank you used to at the very least get a sign-on bonus. You may even have been able to use such an offer to win yourself a hefty pay rise to stay where you are. One of my girl-friends working on the sell side happened to be holiday on bonus day. While lying on the beach she mentioned to her husband that she wasn't sorry to be missing it. The firm had had spectacular results the previous year, but she knew that as a long-serving, loyal member of the company she would never be included in any mass handouts. Her husband told her to stop being so laid back about it and go in and fight her corner. On her arrival back at work the next Monday she was duly given her bonus cheque, a few days after the others. She took the envelope and opened it, noting that she had been given exactly what she expected; a reasonable sum of money, but not one that she felt actually reflected her personal performance or the company's superlative profits the previous year. She returned the cheque to the envelope and pushed it back across the table, telling her boss that she was giving it back to him and asking him to think carefully about her performance the previous year. 'I am not going to hold you to ransom, I am not going to pretend that I am interviewing somewhere else. However, if what you want me to believe is that the firm doesn't rate my capabilities and doesn't consider me to be a key member of staff, then give me back the same cheque next week.' She got up and left the room.

The following week she sat down once more with her boss in the same room. He handed her an envelope again, but this time the size of the cheque inside was much greater. She thanked him and assured him that she was worth every penny. A few days later, a very senior member of the bank stopped her in the corridor. 'I cannot believe,' he said, 'that you could behave so badly.' She looked at him, startled. 'What do you mean?' she asked. 'I understand that you threatened to resign and leave immediately if your bonus was not substantially improved,' he said. Opening her mouth to say that she had threatened nothing of the sort, in fact quite the contrary, she quickly shut it again. It dawned on her that her immediate superior would only have been able to increase the size of her bonus cheque if he had been able to spin a story to the effect that she had threatened to go. So she did not deny the story, but neither did she say that it was true. Let them think what they want, she thought. What matters is that I got the money I deserved.

The point of this story is this: it is only people who scream and shout and threaten to leave who are ever paid properly. Women are just not made like this. By nature they have a greater sense of loyalty to the organisation that employs them.

I count myself among this army of relatively unambitious women. I stayed in one bank for nearly nine years – hardly the way to get paid serious money. And in fact I never *was* paid serious money – it was not until my final year at the bank that I started to receive anything like what I was truly worth to them, let alone anything like my male contemporaries. But it never occurred to me to complain, and certainly not to take them to an industrial tribunal. Why? Because I was very happy doing what I was doing. I had enough money to pay the bills and school fees, and to take some very nice holidays. I had a husband who was contributing to the household income. I thought I was paid adequately, if barely adequately. I also knew the bank very well, and had developed a good understanding of how it worked, and so I was able to achieve my professional objectives much more easily than if I had moved on to a bank where I had to start building an internal network from scratch.

* * *

What about all these well-publicised court cases showing how badly women are treated in the City?

Let's have a look at some of them, starting with Isabelle Terrillon, a broker with Nomura, whose case was heard in March 2001. She was taking on her former employer, claiming that she had been a victim of both sex discrimination and unfair dismissal. The main plank of her argument was that when she had returned from maternity leave in 1998 her job had disappeared.

I have a very un-PC view on maternity leave for which I am regularly reviled by other mothers. However, consider this: how many men in responsible and well-paid jobs do you know who regard taking a holiday of several consecutive weeks as being acceptable? Most of them would baulk at taking two weeks, and even then it would probably be in August, when their clients were also on holiday. If you want to take long holidays, get a job where your responsibilities are well defined in seasonal terms (e.g. teaching) or do as I have done and go into business on your own account, so that if you do decide to take several weeks off and the business suffers as a result, you have let only yourself down. The simple truth is that a five-day-a-week client service job, such as that of a salesperson or trader in the securities markets, does not allow for long periods away from the office.

However, Ms Terrillon took, as was her right, several weeks off following the birth of her child. At the tribunal she sought to add strength to her argument by describing Nomura in less than flattering terms. She accused her former employer of sanctioning a trading floor where male colleagues would make comments such as 'Of all the women on the trading floor, X is the one I'd most like to fuck'. She also alleged that she was sexually harassed by her bosses, who asked her to wear 'short, tight skirts', and that during a client meeting she was asked to strip down and give one of her clients a massage. When she showed displeasure she was asked whether she was going to start crying.

Now I do not deny that trading floors are crass and vulgar places at the best of times, but I would suggest that any workplace that employs large numbers of men, many with limited intellectual capability, would be equally sexist. I recall standing near an attractive female colleague wearing a reasonably short skirt as she leaned across a trading desk to hand some papers to someone on the other side. A male colleague of ours, who was standing behind me, watched appreciatively and then said to her in a completely audible voice that at that moment he had felt the urge to 'slip her on like a wellington boot'. Neither she nor I reached for the phone to call Personnel or our lawyers – frankly this type of comment is par for the course. In fact, my recollection is that she laughed. My advice to those who wish to avoid these kinds of comments is to work in a different environment.

Ms Terillon eventually dropped her claim of sexual discrimination and accepted a sum of money, reportedly £70,000, for unfair dismissal. I have no idea what she is doing now, but I suspect that any employer would think twice before taking on someone who had litigated in this way.

If you must go to court, make sure you win enough money to support yourself for a while out of the workplace. One such award was made recently to Julie Bower, a beverage industry equity analyst who sued her former employer, Schroder Salomon Smith Barney. The case, having opened in the autumn of 2001, was eventually concluded in June 2002. Ms Bower claimed that she had been the victim of sex discrimination resulting from differential bonus payments, leading to forced resignation, and was therefore also seeking compensation for unfair dismissal. She alleged that her bonus of £25,000 for one particular year was 'insultingly' low in comparison to those of two male colleagues who received £650,000 and £450,000. Her argument was that £25,000 was not the market rate for an analyst, was not a realistic valuation of her performance, and that her work was undervalued because she was a woman. She also claimed that she was told during an appraisal in 1999 that she was the worst-performing team leader, when in fact she was ranked 37 out of 68.

To the outside world, Schroders Securities (as it was known at the time of her employment) can't have sounded any more fun than Nomura to work in. At the tribunal, evidence was heard that Ms Bower, who in 1997 underwent ovarian cancer treatment, shortly after her move to Schroders, had been described by one of her managers in the following terms: 'had cancer, been a pain, now pregnant'. In their defence, Schroders argued that Ms Bower was very 'aggressive, arrogant and unhinged'.

That's quite a statement to make about anyone, but as someone who at one stage had responsibility, albeit not for long, for 500 equity analysts, I feel qualified to say that almost all of them at one time or another were capable of displaying aggressive, arrogant and unhinged behaviour – some of them all three. I am not alone in my views; talking to a senior City figure, a former employer of Ms Bower's prior to her time at Schroders, I discovered that he had been invited to give evidence against her at the tribunal. He told me that he had declined, on the basis that even if he agreed with the contention that she was difficult to manage, so was almost everyone else he employed – difficult analysts, like sexist trading floors, are ubiquitous. That is the nature of the City.

The length of the case and the extensive details revealed in court gave the tribunal a better than average opportunity to comment on City practices. They noted that it was 'hard to envisage a process more lacking in transparency' than the bonus-setting system, and their view of the figure of £25,000 was that it was 'picked out of thin air'. Well, I've got news for them, as revealed in my discussion of bonuses in the chapter on pay – so are all bonuses in the City. They also decided that the figure was intended purely to let Ms Bower know that she was not wanted, and that she had been subjected to 'attacks on her personality, character and working ability'.

Ms Bower's case was pursued because the Equal Opportunities Commission had taken it up and fought it on her behalf as a test case. It is unlikely that she would have been able to fund such a prolonged campaign from her own resources – especially given bonuses of £25,000! Schroders refuted her allegations and appealed the tribunal decision, but in the end settled out of court for £1.4 million in compensation on the grounds that the whole case was taking up too much management time.

Deborah Somerville-Cotton was another woman in the City trying to show that maternity leave had ruined her career. A director in treasury products and head of the forward rate agreements (FRA) desk at Barclays Capital, she returned to work to discover that her job had disappeared, and she had been allocated another that she felt was not comparable. This was just after Barclays Capital had lost its shirt on Russian bonds following that country's decision to default on its debt in the middle of an economic crisis, so it's perhaps not surprising that there had to be a bit of restructuring. In fact Mrs Somerville-Cotton was the only individual retained from the FRA desk after the restructuring, with all those laid off being male. Perhaps they should have brought a claim for sex discrimination!

She didn't succeed – the tribunal found against her, both at first sitting and appeal. They described Barclays Capital's actions as 'legitimate restructuring'. I'm not surprised.

JP Morgan claimed that they had been undertaking a bit of legitimate restructuring when they laid off Aisling Sykes, a lawyer and vice-president of the Transaction Execution Group, who already had three children and was pregnant with the fourth at the time, although this last fact was unknown to JP Morgan. Ms Sykes claimed unfair dismissal and sex discrimination.

It was explained in court that Sykes had requested flexible working hours on numerous occasions. This had been accommodated to the extent that she was required in the office between 9 a.m. and 6.15 p.m., and to work from home after 7.30 p.m., having put the children to bed.

Do these hours sound onerous to you? They sound perfectly normal to me, even a bit lax. I cannot remember having the luxury of starting at 9 a.m. in the whole nine years I worked in the City, even during my stints in corporate finance. I recall that during my time pregnant with son number two, then living in Hong Kong, I was prone to tiredness in the afternoons and used to go home for a two-hour nap. I returned to work at 4 p.m. just as Europe was waking up and then went home again at 7.30 p.m. for dinner before working on through the European day. I mention this not to make me out to be a martyr or hard done by; if you are working for a bank where all the decisions are made in a different time zone, and you want to make things happen, you have no choice but to work around the clock. If hours are an issue for you, choose to work on the buy side, where you will start later and finish earlier than you would on the sell side.

I am frequently told by women in senior jobs who have had a baby that they long to return to work part-time and plan to ask their employer whether they may do so. My advice to them is – don't! The minute you ask to work part-time it will be assumed that you are less committed than you were. Instead, work full-time but keep your diary clear one day a week and spend that day at home. However, remember that working at home does not mean looking after children at home – you will still need childcare support five days a week. Also remember that working part-time will probably mean accepting a lesser role and therefore less money, so the economics may not work out either.

A request for flexible hours certainly didn't help Aisling Sykes. She claimed that it led to her superiors forming the view that she had lost energy, motivation and focus. Eventually, in November 1998, Sykes was called to a meeting with no prior notice and made redundant; she was informed that the decision was not performance based.

Sykes claimed that her dismissal was unlawful sex discrimination. She also claimed that JP Morgan's initial refusal to accommodate her request for flexible working arrangements was itself a form of indirect sex discrimination. As regards her dismissal, she asserted that it was procedurally unfair.

JP Morgan gave redundancy as the reason for the admitted dismissal of Sykes. She had not been selected for redundancy on the grounds of her sex, it was asserted, and they had not known of her pregnancy at the time. In addition, Sykes's initial requests for more flexible working arrangements had been accommodated. Sex discrimination was denied.

On the fourth day of the original hearing, JP Morgan admitted that the dismissal had been procedurally unfair. The tribunal found that she had not been unfairly discriminated against, and Sykes then appealed against this decision.

On appeal, the tribunal found partly in her favour. For all her efforts in bringing the sex discrimination case all the way to appeal, she was awarded the princely sum of £12,000. As far as the late hours being a form of indirect discrimination were concerned, the appeal court did not find in her favour. They said that there was no reason for her not to comply, and that the requirement was justified on grounds irrespective of sex, particularly in relation to work carried out on deals in other time zones.

Kay Swinburne worked at Deutsche Bank and sued them for sexual discrimination in January 2000 because she claimed that they had failed to prevent a 'hostile environment'. Now my idea of a hostile environment is when you've gone out on a limb to recommend a stock to numerous clients, lots of them have bought it, and then the share price completely collapses. Ms Swinburne's hostile environment was, she claimed, nurtured by her boss, who made sexist comments which ultimately led to her resignation from her £300,000 job.

Deutsche Bank, as described in this case, sounds to me like any other collection of under-educated men, rather as Nomura did in the case mentioned above. The tribunal may have been surprised to hear (I was not) that male staff organised escort girls to attend a Christmas party and one of the managers frequently referred to women as 'hot totty', 'birds' or 'chicks'.

I guess that Deutsche's defence that this was just 'office banter' was probably initially correct. Somewhere down the line things got out of hand, and when, as Ms Swinburne claimed, juniors were encouraged to laugh at her by the senior manager, therefore depriving her of her integrity, and she was also accused by her boss of sleeping with a client, she decided that enough was enough. So did the tribunal. They found in her favour, but before compensation could be awarded Deutsche settled out of court for a rumoured £500,000.

Finally there is the case of Louise Barton, a former highly rated media analyst with Investec Henderson Crosthwaite, who brought a complaint of sex discrimination against her employer on the grounds of differential remuneration. She had recruited Mathew Horsman, a journalist, to join her team, and claimed that over a four-year period she received about half the pay and bonuses he did, despite producing similar revenues – £11.5 million. Barton received £1.1 million over the period in question while Horsman received £2.2 million.

Barton also argued that when she was originally recruiting Horsman, an agreement had been reached to take a collegiate approach and pool bonuses. In 1998 they both received £50,000, but in March 2000 Ms Barton was given £115,000 while Mr Horsman received £350,000. She also claimed that he was not an outstanding performer and had to be helped in order to get a deal off the ground.

Investec argued that the difference in bonus was due purely to material factors and not gender, something that Barton disputed, as she did figures showing Horsman's higher productivity. Investec's view was that, in the year to March 2000, Mr Horsman had generated three to four times as much revenue as Ms Barton, and in the year to March 2001 twice as much. Investec's chairman, Perry Crosthwaite, went so far as to state that Mr Horsman was 'one of the two or three high profile characters' in the bank and could help secure the firm's future.

The fact that headhunters had targeted Mr Horsman was used by Investec, who said that this justified the incentives paid to him to stay. In addition, they said that Ms Barton was simply resentful because Horsman had grown to be more successful than her. The tribunal found for Investec, holding that it was a vital component of the City bonus culture that bonuses were discretionary and individuals' bonuses were not revealed, except when requested by the court. This was rather a different comment on bonuses to that in the Julie Bower case, the outcome of which had presumably encouraged Louise Barton to bring hers.

Louise Barton, at the time of going to press, had won the right to a fresh hearing. Born in rural Australia, she had this to say about trading floors:

> The only difference between a shearing shed and a trading floor is that men in a shearing shed wear singlets and on the trading floor they wear suits. The people are equally coarse.

I couldn't agree more, Louise.

We could examine many more cases, but I am sure that you get the picture by now. The City is a sexist place because there are more men than women working there, and as long as finance remains a global twenty-four-hour game that will always be the case. The rewards may be high, but the angst you will have to endure as a woman in the Square Mile may not be worth it. And it is almost certainly never a good idea to go to court.

* * *

One way to survive in the City as a woman is to make sure that you never venture from the building without the proper kit – in other words, a correctly stocked handbag. First, you have to resolve the whole handbag/briefcase debate. Should you carry both a briefcase and a handbag (a lot to lug around), a briefcase with no handbag (where do you put your purse, your lipstick, etc.?) or a handbag with no briefcase (meaning you will have to carry the research notes you are going to present in your hand). This is massively irritating, and my current answer is to use a beautiful Gucci handbag that accommodates A4-size documents and even my laptop when it needs to.

Most Socially Acceptable Girlfriend and I used to go out on client forays as a pair on regular occasions, targeting them with what we described as our 'pincer movement'. MSAG is the most organised person I know and would always be well equipped when going on a client visit. The usual requirements (pens, a notebook, diary, business cards, the client's address and even a map, multiple copies of the research we were going to present) would be accompanied by those needed by City women on the move. A small hairbrush, a lipstick and a compact were the main make-up staples. A WAP-enabled mobile telephone for use when visiting Scottish fund managers and getting stranded in Edinburgh after the last flight had gone was also essential. MSAG would also always have a mouth-freshener spray, for those days when we had drunk late into the night with clients or taken them out for a curry or a Chinese. Halitosis is not helpful when you are trying to get as close to your client as possible. A spare pair – or two – of tights is essential, because nothing matters more than first impressions. Finally, don't forget your company credit card.

Make the most of being in the minority. Use the fact that you have to spend hours being nice to senior corporate clients or institutional fund managers by treating them as attractive men, even if they look like the back end of a bus. It works wonders – trust me, I know. This is not the time to get on your high horse and say that you wish to be treated equally – let them open doors for you, help you on with your coat, offer you the coffee first. You will win more corporate broker-ships, more deals and generate more commission if you flutter your eyelashes a little. Personal presentation matters if you are going to use being female to its best advantage.

Much of what I know on this subject I learned from my Most Glamorous Girlfriend, when we both worked in an advertising agency early in my career. Once we had worked next door to each other for a while I realised that MGG took herself off to the loo several times a day for what seemed to me extended periods of time. Initially concerned about her bladder, and too young and naive to suspect that she was snorting cocaine, I followed her in there one day and discov-ered her secret – she religiously reapplied her make-up several times a day. Even now, seventeen years later, I strug-gle to manage much more than tinted moisturiser and a bit of lipstick, so this was a revelation. I stood next to her in the Ladies, watching and learning how to use a make-up sponge, why you need different brushes for lips and cheeks, how to camouflage bags under the eyes and irritating post-adolescent spots. Excellent training for someone who later had to learn how to use being a woman to good effect to survive in a man's world. Especially when it was necessary to apply the chocolate knickers treatment, described at the end of Chapter 2. I can think of nowhere else, other than possibly down a coal mine, where women are still such a rarity. If you are a woman, and work in the City, use it to your advantage. Plenty of us have.

Chapter 7

Sex in the City

Sex in the City

THIS IS THE CHAPTER THAT several former colleagues are dreading. They can relax. My ex-boyfriends can cancel any plans for a class-action lawsuit. Everyone who has ever suggested having an affair with me (where do they think I am going to find the time, let alone the inclination?) can stop worrying. This is not going to be a list of personal anecdotes from the bedroom.

When the then editor of the weekend *FT* first contacted me to ask me to be a columnist in the now defunct *Business* magazine, it was not to write Mrs Moneypenny. Rather, she was after a weekly offering on the subject of sex in the workplace. I told her that, while I was flattered to be asked, I didn't think that it was really my cup of tea. I was at that time living and working in Japan for a bank that employed something over 70,000 people worldwide; I explained to the editor that not only had I never had sex in any of our offices, to the best of my knowledge I hadn't had sex with anyone who worked in the organisation. Well, she said, what about sexual harassment? I told her that I wished it were even remotely possible – I weighed far too much and would be very unlikely to draw the attentions, unwanted or otherwise, of my male colleagues. Sexual discrimination? The glass ceiling? I confessed to not having noticed whether one existed. I then went on to explain that sex wasn't a high priority for me given my various responsibilities, namely three children, 220 employees, a PhD thesis, and so on. It was then that she suggested I write a column about my life instead. Much simpler.

Of course, it never fails to amaze me that anyone working in the City ever finds time for sex. Those who know the birthdays of my three sons will realise that I myself only manage to have sex once a year. I recently met up with one of my girlfriends who still works in the City. She was bemoaning the fact that her husband had recently bought her a book – not just any book, but one designed to rev up their love life. She spends half of every week flying around continental Europe, and she told him that the book was completely impractical. It had far too much text. The time available to her to read documents that were not prospectuses, company financials or press releases was very limited, and if he wanted her to read a whole book on sex he had better find one with lots of pictures.

I don't believe that the real story about sex in the City concerns relationships between consenting adults in the workplace, although there are of course plenty of those. Here, though, the City is no different from any other work environment. Wherever people work long hours, barely see their wives, travel extensively and consume alcohol regularly, and are generally over-paid, you will find plenty of illicit (and non-illicit) relationships. I'm not a big fan of extramarital relationships; I have never known them end in anything other than tears, and divorce in my opinion is a massively overrated pastime and probably the fastest way to penury. The investment banker who chooses to station his family miles out in the country and keep a bachelor pad for the week is asking for trouble, and I have seen this scenario end badly on several occasions. Equally I know several couples in the City who have worked together, gone out together, got married and continued to work together (sometimes even sitting next to each other for years) and are perfectly happy.

Extramarital affairs in the City, with a few rare exceptions, simply do not come to the attention of the public in the same way that, say, those of politicians or TV stars do. They are just not of interest to the average guy in the street, simply because the people involved are not famous. The one exception I can think of is the man the *Sunday Mirror* described as the 'six hundred million pound bonker', a reference to one of Nick Leeson's (of Barings fame) bosses, who had left home to set up with someone else's wife.

Of much more concern to me than extramarital affairs is the whole matter of post-coital etiquette (PCE), on which I hold strong views. I remember as if it were yesterday letting a female member of the sales team in my care, who was very much the worse for wear, go home in the early hours with a predatory fund manager who was one of our clients. I consoled myself with the thought that they were both single and over the age of consent. The next day she still made the morning meeting, although clearly deprived of sleep. By 11 a.m., when no evidence of correct PCE had materialised, I could not contain myself any longer and called him. These men need to learn some manners. Did he not think that, following an overnight stay, a thank-you might be a good idea? I asked. He must have taken my words to heart because less than an hour later a suitable bouquet arrived at her desk. He has since married and retired, and I know that she has also married and may have left the City as well. But I wonder whether she ever realised why she got those flowers?

One aspect of sex in the City that does make the papers regularly is the subject of lap-dancing, or table-dancing, clubs. Acres of newsprint have been given over to describing bankers visiting establishments such as Stringfellows or Spearmint Rhino. The sums of money involved are reported to reach ludicrous proportions. Here I can claim some first-hand knowledge, and can confirm that the sums do indeed have several zeros on the end. I know for a fact that one manager in an investment bank in London signed off a £7,000 expense claim, the only piece of supporting evidence for which was a table napkin with 'received, £7,000 for dinner services' written on it.

Understand that I do not condone lap-dancing clubs, or even think them a necessary pastime for career advancement in the financial services sector. There are many successful people in the City who have never been near such a place. In fact, let's be even more specific – most people in the City have never been near such a place. It is just that the ones who do go get plenty of publicity.

So what goes on in these places? In comparison to other parts of the world, London's lap-dancing establishments are tame. They essentially maintain a no-contact environment, and as a result are a lot cheaper than their counterparts in, for example, the Far East. Getting into them is not prohibitively expensive – in most cases the clubs have a £15–30 entrance fee, which includes a complimentary drink. Then the meter starts running.

After being seated you are usually told that you have to order a bottle of champagne for the table: prices start at £90. I am informed that girls then start 'preying on you like vultures' for a table dance. It costs £10 a song for a girl to dance topless at your table. Private dances in the 'special section' cost approximately £20 a song, and here the girls will remove all their clothes. But as someone said to me, 'You are shown everything but there is no touching. The closest you are going to get is a nipple brushed a hair's breath from your face.' The special section is usually in a dimly lit room with armchairs that are positioned so that clients can't see the look on each other's faces. Masturbation is not tolerated and will lead to the bouncer (there is one always watching out for trouble) escorting you from the premises in a less than gentle manner.

Handing over large sums of money for a voyeuristic experience that you could get by paying a slightly higher satellite television fee or raiding the top rack of magazines in any newsagent is understandably rather frustrating, no doubt in the physical as well as the psychological sense. It is also erroneous to describe the activity as 'lap-dancing' – the 'no contact' rule means that if a girl were really on your lap she'd need to be able to float.

Back at your table, the girls will offer to sit next to you and be 'yours' for £150 an hour. This is a substantial multiple of the minimum wage, and it is not difficult to see why nurses, teachers, out-of-work actresses and the like are all to be found in lap-dancing establishments. I have it on the best authority, though, that this rate is negotiable. One equity salesman told me, 'My best rate was zero. I cut a deal with her that if she espied someone who might pay more, she could leave the table at any time. In the meantime, there was always the chance that my client might ask her for a dance.' It never fails to amaze me that more of these boys – who are, after all, ruthless in negotiation during the day when they have to make prices and take trading positions – don't haggle more over these extortionate charges.

Because they are all working on commission, girls in most London strip clubs are very pushy. My informants tell me that it can be hard to relax with girls forming queues to your table and using any means at their disposal to persuade you of your need for one or more private dances. Apparently an establishment called Metropolis, located in Bethnal Green, has filled a gap in the market for a less aggressive lap-dancing club. At Metropolis the girls will wander by, smile and await an invitation to join your table. If no such invitation is forthcoming, they keep on walking. This strategy seems to work – my field research team all tell me that they always seem to end up paying for more table dances at Metropolis than anywhere else. Another feature of Metropolis worth mentioning – simply as an observation on how they have sought to gain a competitive advantage through diversification – is the shower room. Here the girls soap themselves in an erotic fashion and the customers get a water gun each with which to spray them. Showers, like private dances, cost £20 per person, and clients consider that by London standards this is money well spent.

Japan, where I spent two years signing expense claims from lap-dancing clubs, is at the other end of the spectrum. Clubs in the Tokyo district of Roppongi are mostly geared toward the *gaijin* (foreigner) clientele. For the most part these clubs employ foreign girls, from everywhere imaginable – New Zealand, Africa, the Netherlands, Bolivia, Portugal and the Solomon Islands, for a start. Establishments frequented by the over-paid, over-sexed expatriate investment bankers include ones with such exotic names as 7th Heaven and Climax.

Entry into one of these clubs costs around ¥5,000 per person. This is generally negotiable with larger groups and/or 'good customer' – i.e. frequent user – status. You are seated in the main area in view of several chrome poles with girls dancing around them. Customers are encouraged to stuff cash or 'heavenly money' – essentially a scam whereby ¥1,000 denominations in fake money can be purchased for a 20 per cent mark-up on the equivalent in real cash – into a girl's knickers for an obligatory return 'facial', in other words being smothered in her breasts.

Girls will come around and try to sweet-talk their way onto your lap in the hope of tempting you with a private lap-dance conducted in a cordoned-off area, usually at the back of the room, with 'discretion' in mind. The girls pay the house around ¥21,000 (US$170) per evening to work there; they are entitled to keep 80 per cent of any revenue that they generate over and above this amount. A private dance lasts approximately three to five minutes, depending on the song. In that time your chosen lady will perform an erotic dance during which I am told that you are allowed to fondle, suck or nibble any part of her except her southern regions. (It is amazing how often visitors end up with a cold the day after, presumably caught from the previous customer.) The dance sets you back ¥7,000 a song. One broker told me, 'One client outing, with several fund managers in tow, set me back a hundred and forty dances. One of them went for thirty-five straight dances!' The clubs process payment every time an individual private dance session is concluded, rather than presenting the whole tab at the end of the evening, presumably to guard against a credit card having reached its limit. To avoid detection you can pay in cash – all these establishments have a supply of printed receipts purporting to be from Chinese restaurants, wine bars and so on which they will happily date as required. But in Japan entertaining is such a way of life that generally no one bats an eyelid when the time comes for these expeditions to be accounted for back in the office.

For those with more adventurous tastes, there are bondage clubs. Sugar Heel is probably the most well known in Roppongi. Here an equity salesman may have to handcuff his client to a dominatrix, which is one way to make sure that more orders come his way. These clubs actively seek customer participation, although you do have a choice as to whether you want to be *Sado* (sadist) or *Maso* (masochist). The Sugar Heel performers apparently really get stuck in, and the whips, chains, ropes and candle wax are fully utilised. There is no play-acting at all, and even those with a high tolerance to violence will wince watching the spectacle.

Tokyo being the city it is, there is plenty of choice. One club, Regina, is a halfway house, blending bondage and karaoke. I asked one of my researchers to describe how it worked. 'I was in there one night out with a very good friend and client of mine. We were drinking beer and singing karaoke as happy drunks. No sooner had we started singing "Strangers in the Night" than a Japanese gentleman was dragged into the main area tied and bound like an animal prepared for a spit roast. He was bound so tightly that his wedding tackle was exposed. The dominatrix then removed one of her shoes and proceeded to whack the protruding organ with the sole of her shoe. We were completely speechless. In fact, no sooner had we realised what she was about to do than we both had our hands on our own tackle and were in danger of dislocated jaws. The whole spectacle brought tears to our eyes and we hurriedly left to spend the rest of the evening in a more sedate establishment.'

In Hong Kong the Wanchai district is the main centre for strip clubs. While they operate fundamentally in the same way as those in London and Tokyo, the difference is that they try to sell you additional 'services'. Not just private dances or expensive drinks – the works. The idea at the end of the night is to order 'takeout' with the girl you fancy, which will set you back US$200–400, payable to the mama-san, who takes her cut. The earlier you purchase your takeout, the more it will cost, as you have to compensate the club for loss of the girl's services.

Hong Kong is littered with clubs that could politely be called 'pit stops', where the one thing on offer, oral sex, is performed in a swift and businesslike fashion. They are intended for the businessman who has wined and dined his client and wants a brief sexual interlude before they go on to the next round of lagers. It usually costs about US$50 per 'job'.

The one place where I have seen the inside of girlie clubs more often than I have had to sign off expenses from them was in the Philippines. I started travelling there on business in the mid-1990s, just after Manila had been cleaned up and all these establishments relocated to one specific street. Here most places operated private rooms at the back and charged exorbitant drink prices at the bar; 'takeout' was available, but again was much cheaper if you waited until the place closed. The street had become almost a tourist destination in its own right, and occasionally a client or a colleague of mine would want to visit out of sheer curiosity if nothing else. I would wander in with them, the only woman in the place not for sale, and sit chatting to the girls, who at least all spoke good English and were usually highly educated. Many that I met were doctors, university lecturers and the like – these clubs really are a stark illustration of the free market at its worst. Wages are so low in places like the Philippines and Indonesia that, having qualified as a paediatrician, say, you are better off finding work sitting beside an overweight investment banker, stroking the inside of his leg while he conducts a highly boring conversation with his colleague, probably (if they are, say, German, Dutch or French) in a language you don't understand.

All these places prosper and thrive because of the money spent by people in the financial services industry. Of course, people from other walks of life end up in strip clubs from time to time, but the City still supplies the largest proportion of customers. Why? As an industry it breeds men who work long hours, have large and often fragile egos, and are well paid. There is no quicker fix for flagging self-esteem than the attention of a pretty girl – and it can be had for £10 less than fifteen minutes by taxi from the office. When work is stressful, whether that stress is real or imagined, letting your hair down in a strip club is one way to relax, I suppose. From a professional point of view, if the client wants to go to these places and the salesman is happy to take him, then it is a worthwhile exercise. I have signed off expenses for both fund management and corporate clients, and seen real financial payback from both. In both instances they would have been people who were entertained by such a visit, and as a result of it became closer to the salesman or corporate finance executive who hosted them. In the case of fund management clients this almost always led to a 'thank you' order being directed to our bank the next morning, in value many multiples of what we had spent on him the night before. This level of return on capital employed, as it were, means that the commercial argument for taking fund managers to strip clubs is compelling – assuming that they wish to go. Even hosting the finance directors and chief executives of public companies is worthwhile – the more closely they bond with the bank's staff, the more likely they are to maintain a relationship with the bank, which will be able to charge large sums next time they need to raise capital or be advised on an acquisition or disposal.

Not every fund manager or director of a public company needs or wants to be taken to a club where female attention is on offer and the female body is displayed. Most of them, as it happens, could think of nothing worse. The best client/broker relationships develop when the two individuals have something in common, such as a shared love of cricket or the opera, and much money continues to be spent on entertaining clients in boxes at Lord's or Covent Garden. This may be more acceptable in your eyes than the likes of Stringfellows or Spearmint Rhino, but it is exactly the same principle. The City is first and foremost a relationship industry, and one in which to some extent the consumer is indifferent to price. Corporate clients would no more shop around for the best price for advice than fly to the moon. Can you imagine planning a bid for Safeway and then calling round the City trying to get the best possible price for the advice? The confidentiality issues alone would be horrendous – it would be out in the market in five minutes. Since lowering prices is not an available strategy, as it would be in any other industry, building and sustaining relationships through entertaining is all-important.

* * *

How did I survive in an industry where I was having to subsidise the strip clubs of the world? The answer is by being objective – as long as I was not asked to do anything I didn't enjoy personally, and as long as it was genuinely resulting in more business for the bank, then I didn't get worked up about it. I don't much care for Wagner and cannot think of anything likely to induce me to sit through a performance of the *Ring*, but if someone working for me wanted to do so and take a client with them, at £200 a ticket plus dinner at another £100 or so a head, so be it. I would always check the commission figures for that client over the next day or so, however he had been entertained.

I happen to think that the world would be a better place without all these opportunities for wasting money, whether personal or the company's, on various degrees of sexual gratification. But as far as I was concerned, if it was legal and it made money that was fine.

How to survive if you end up having to go to one of these places and have never been before, or would rather not be there? Do as I do and treat the whole thing as a spectacle, like a stage show where you happen to be sitting on the stage rather than in the audience. Show the girls respect and speak to them as equals – you have no right to take the moral high ground, you have no idea about their personal circumstances. And, above all, observe Chatham House rules. Just because you know that a member of your managing board, or your most senior client, bought a girl out and took her home does not give you carte blanche to mention it to him, or indeed anyone else, at a later date. The whole experience was a dream – it never happened.

Chapter 8

Working Overseas

Working Overseas

THE CITY IS, AS I SAID earlier, more a way of life than a physical place. Moving money around is not an activity confined to the City of London, to postcodes starting with EC. Fund managers and stockbrokers and other kinds of people involved with money are present in large numbers in many other parts of the world. When I was a London-based stockbroker I had to speak to fund managers and even companies who were based overseas on a regular basis, and visit them from time to time. I was as fascinated by the movement of money in New York, Sydney, Singapore, Hong Kong and Tokyo (and even Des Moines, Iowa) as much as I was by the same activity in London. So when I was offered the chance to work abroad, I jumped at it. During my time at the bank, I was sent to Hong Kong (for two years), Singapore (for nine months) and finally to Tokyo, where I had the most senior and responsible job of my career for almost two years. I survived all these overseas jaunts, but they presented their own challenges over and above the ones I had already encountered.

Seven months pregnant and without a word of Japanese – that's how I arrived in Tokyo to take up my new job in October 1998. The job itself was pretty undefined, at least in the eyes of the man I had notionally come to work for. Our only previous meeting had been a couple of weeks earlier at breakfast in a London hotel. Now I was sitting in front of him receiving my instructions. He had an office that was large and also largely empty. The desk was immaculate. 'So,' he said, 'what can you do?'

What I could do, as it turned out, was run the office very efficiently on his behalf. Looking back on the whole experience, I am amazed that I dared roll up my sleeves and get stuck in to the day-to-day business of running an investment bank in Tokyo. But at the time I was quite clearly suffering from delusions brought on no doubt by the raging hormones of my advanced state of pregnancy. I readily agreed to tackle his problems one at a time until they were all resolved.

We couldn't have been more different. I was a white, over-educated Protestant girl in her late thirties who was the product of a comfortable middle-class upbringing. He came from a poor Catholic Irish family who emigrated a generation before his birth, and he hadn't bothered with as much further education as I had. He used to joke with me that MBA was a common title in our office, but whereas mine had been obtained through hard grind in the lecture theatres and library of the London Business School, everyone else's stood for Married But Available. We had both married foreigners (him a Japanese, me an Australian) and both had three sons, but mine spoke English and his Japanese.

The real reasons behind my arrival in Tokyo, and more specifically in his office, were a little (but not much) more thought out than they might at first appear. Mr M, fed up with his job in Singapore working for a vast media empire, had agreed to set up a Japanese office for that selfsame empire. I had always loved Japan, had been there regularly over the years on business, and adored Japanese food. I was working in Singapore too, but the combination of the end of my assignment and the imminent arrival of our third child had led me to seek a sabbatical from the bank, which I planned to spend quietly in Japan working on my long-overdue PhD thesis. However, this was not to be. The bank had recently promoted one of my favourite managers to the stratosphere and given him its worldwide equities business to develop. In the first month of my sabbatical, this demigod put it to me that, as I was going to be in Japan anyway, why didn't I spend a few days a week helping to get things under control?

Things needed to be under control. October 1999 was only a year away, and there was much to do. In that month Japan was scheduled to have its own Big Bang. For those of you too young to remember or too ignorant of the ways of the Square Mile, this was an event that took place in the UK in 1986 and in the USA in 1978. Despite Japan being built on a major fault line, the term Big Bang did not refer to a seismic incident but to the ending of fixed commissions in the financial marketplace. Up until that date, every investor, be he (or she) small or large, individual or institution, paid the same percentage commission for buying and selling stocks and shares. In Japan there was a scale of charges according to size, but the average commission paid for onshore transactions stood at just over 100 basis points (bank-speak for 1 per cent). This represented, in 1998, less than one-fifth of the typical charge paid by fund managers in Europe or the US. While our little operation was steadily growing its revenue, it was clear that four-fifths of it was likely to disappear overnight in a year's time.

Two things were going to happen as a consequence of Big Bang. One was that many small stockbrokers would go to the wall as the margins in the business disappeared. The other was that many foreign investors who had previously settled their share-buying transactions offshore to avoid the high charges would now move onshore and probably set up operations there. Both of these dynamics would change the face of stockbroking in Japan for ever. And I was going to be there when it happened.

When it eventually did happen, stockbrokers in Japan finally had to face what most of the world had had to for years – the fact that fund management clients could and would use their strength to pay minimal commissions. After a year of playing Cassandra, and lecturing my colleagues at every opportunity about the implications of this for our P&L, it was marginally satisfying to see commissions fall from over 100 basis points to less than 20. At least, it would have been if it hadn't also meant that we had to put our foot on the accelerator to make up for the income drop.

My boss had joined the bank as an outsider after many years' service at another financial institution, most of them in Tokyo. He was in many ways the typical expat-gone-native. Married to a Japanese wife, he lived an hour away by bullet train and his three children attended Japanese schools. His temper was legendary, and woe betide the secretary that forgot that he didn't like mustard in his hamburgers. We made an odd couple but soon learned to play to each other's strengths. Despite his chronic lack of formal education, he was the commensurate host, father figure and office leader, with good Japanese language skills and an understanding of how the industry was regulated. I made up for his deficiencies in the understanding of financials and the writing of business plans. I also knew what our head office, far away in Europe, would tolerate and what it would not. In this way we managed to run the office together, allowing him to go for regular golf lessons and me to spend large chunks of the school holidays overseas.

Long hours in the office mean that every moment of sleep counts. I worked out when in Tokyo that if I allocated a specific amount of time for each task that I was supposed to undertake every day, I needed seventeen hours. That left seven hours a day for sleep, meals, having a shower and going to the loo. The Japanese, however, were a great example of how to make the most of every day. They seem to have perfected the art of catnapping anywhere at any time.

The lengthy commutes that most Japanese working in Tokyo are forced to endure should, in theory, provide an excellent opportunity to catch up on lost sleep. However, there are precious few seats and almost everybody has to stand. At one point I was shown the latest invention – a device resembling a tall music stand with a headrest, allowing one to rest one's head while standing on the train. The height is adjustable, so presumably the manufacturers were hoping to develop an export market.

Whether they commute or not, most Japanese carry handkerchiefs with them. These are not used to blow one's nose – blowing one's nose in public, and particularly in restaurants, is the height of rudeness in Japan. Rather, the handkerchiefs are used to dab their brows in order to mop up excessive perspiration. The packed trains and constant moving up and down stairs and escalators at stations mean that most *sararimen* arrive at work covered in sweat, whatever the time of year.

* * *

Bowing technique is very important in Japan, and I never did really grasp its finer points. For day-to-day greetings among one's peer group, a brief inclination of the head and the top of the shoulders seems acceptable. When saying 'thank you', the shoulders have to drop farther. For greeting senior people, or on being introduced to them, a much deeper bow is necessary. An apology is a ninety-degree job, and a mega apology (e.g. a company going bankrupt, or a nuclear accident) demands that you kneel down and touch your forehead to the floor. I was much aided in my understanding of bowing by the graduate training handbook of a Japanese investment bank I came across. As well as bowing positions, it also had helpful sections on serving tea, clearing up ashtrays and, when travelling to a client meeting, where to sit in a taxi (in the front) or in a private car (in the middle at the back).

At one point I helped to host a lunch for Ian Macfarlane, the Governor of the Reserve Bank of Australia, at which several senior Japanese clients were present. Having spent the previous twenty minutes bowing, I carried on even when introduced to Mr Macfarlane. No doubt senior Australian central bankers think this is perfectly usual behaviour in middle-aged female English investment bankers. In deference to his seniority, I bowed very low. My boss, who was behind me, reminded me that my legs didn't bear any resemblance to Elle Macpherson's and perhaps I had better start wearing longer skirts.

* * *

I was working in Japan at a time when recruiting and retaining staff were horribly difficult. I used to think that Russia represented the worst aspects of a free market out of control, but that was before I tried to hire people in what looked like (but turned out not to be!) the start of an economic recovery in Japan. The shortage of investment analysts in Tokyo even made a headline in the *FT* in September 1999, reinforcing my experience that the mismatch between supply and demand was not just driving up prices but making it impossible to hire. During my entire stint in Japan there was never a point at which the office headcount was at full strength.

Japan is a major financial centre and English is the medium of communication required for marketing and doing business internationally. However, operating without a knowledge of Japanese is impossible for people involved in the analysis of companies. It's true to say that the Japanese speak English far better and in much greater numbers than English-speakers manage Japanese, but to find someone who is a good analyst *and* a good linguist proved to be a needle-in-a-haystack job. It also hurts to have to pay telephone-number figures for frankly average people. The Japanese have grown up in a culture where unquestioningly obeying instructions is their way of doing things, and initiative is actively discouraged. I just didn't have the time to spell out to people earning more than US$500,000 a year what they should be doing all day.

Importing people from overseas, without Japanese language skills but with a knowledge of trading the Nikkei, was not necessarily a solution to the tight labour market, as I discovered. The Japanese have a lot of respect for pieces of paper, and find it hard to believe that any organisation would be prepared to pay millions of yen to hire someone who left school at sixteen without impressive bits of paper, let alone relocate them plus wife, nanny, children and a forty-foot container from somewhere (usually Essex) over six thousand miles away. I spent many hours patiently explaining that it was exactly this sort of person that, in our opinion, was best suited to trading Japanese stocks. However, it was an unrewarding exercise. I started to think that I was going to have to make it compulsory for all prospective employees to have at least three imposing pieces of paper with them when they moved to Japan. Boy Scout knot-tying certificates would be just fine.

Even if I could successfully persuade the immigration authorities that Boy Scout certificates demonstrated a candidate's strong suitability to trade Japanese shares, I still had to to deal with the regulators in my attempt to use imported labour. Originally I had been encouraged by the fact that, in 1999, for the first time ever, one of the main regulatory authorities was setting its examination in English. As there are no less than four Japanese alphabets, and the main one has over 2,500 characters, this development looked to be extremely promising. However, my joy was somewhat mitigated by hearing that the English set text for the exam retailed at a cool one million yen (a bit less than US$10,000). This really was the free market at work.

Retaining staff was also a challenge; at one point it seemed to me that every executive search firm in Tokyo had access to our internal telephone directory. I once found my boss, who, as mentioned, had lived in Japan for many years and supposedly knew how to deal respectfully with Japanese staff, explaining to a clerk in human resources that any information leak would result in him personally opening the window behind where the poor man sat to facilitate his suicide.

One advantage of the expatriate community being so small was that I could usually rely on meeting the wives of the main movers and shakers in the financial community, and inspecting their clothes and jewellery used to tell me much more than any headhunter could about how good their husbands were at their jobs. One particular wife sported diamond earrings that I swear were well over two carats each, and I knew straight away that not only was her husband an exceptional trader but that we would never be able to afford him.

On one occasion we were raided by the main regulatory authority. We were not known as law-breakers, we had not engaged in any suspicious trades or transactions, it was simply that they were working their way around all the foreign-owned banks and it happened to be our turn. They called up one morning and asked whether it was convenient to start an inspection. When we said 'yes' and enquired when they were due to arrive, it emerged that they were already outside in the corridor. They proceeded to enter and occupy our main meeting room for five weeks. They also requested all our paper records from the last ten years to be removed from archive and brought back to the building for review. The only room big enough to house all the boxes was the staff canteen, which we were obliged by law to provide. At vast expense we then had to resort to renting space in a serviced office suite elsewhere in the building for the lunch-eaters. At the end of this exercise we were formally summoned to be ticked off over two or three minor misdemeanours that seemed to be a matter of interpretation rather than law-breaking, and escaped without a fine or (as is common) a licence suspension. The ticking-off was administered to me in person in Japanese, the senior official pausing every now and then to let the translator go through his paces, despite the fact that everyone around the table spoke perfectly good English.

* * *

Bonus time in investment banks, as I discussed in the chapter on pay, offers an opportunity for managers to spend all night at their desks trying to perform the miracle of the loaves and the fishes. In Tokyo, my HR manager and I would regularly work past midnight trying to reconcile our bonus figures with those issued by head office, as well as undertaking all the currency conversion. This, combined with having to write notification letters for more than 200 people and finalise the payroll before sending it off, was no fun at all.

Depending on your perspective, bonuses are a blessing or a curse. The theory is that in an industry with such volatile earnings, an individual's remuneration is most efficiently used as an incentive when linked with results. In good years the shareholders and the employees share the rewards. In bad years, the wage bill is kept low. The lack of an upper limit is supposed to serve as a strong incentive. In practice, faced with a rising Nikkei and a continual shortage of good bilingual staff, as I was in 1999 and 2000, any investment bank paying out low or zero bonuses is effectively issuing an open invitation to its competitors to poach its people. And of course, those coordinating the worldwide exercise from a desk in western Europe were doing so with no heed paid to the time difference, public holidays or the fact that the Japanese payroll company we used needed a full fourteen working days to process payment.

Calculating bonuses in Japan also requires advanced spreadsheet training. The number of zeros involved is so large that I was constantly having to reformat the column width, and once you instruct the computer to insert the comma that separates the thousands the problem is compounded even further. Then I found myself frantically scrolling over to the left of the spreadsheet to remind myself of the previous year's details, since it would not all fit on the same page. I now know why my colleagues in Spain and Italy were so delighted to adopt the euro.

On top of this there is the problem of having to remember which Suzuki is which. The Japanese use very few surnames and Suzuki is the most common, accounting for some 20 per cent of the population. People in Japan are always called by their surnames, so Suzuki-san the driver is addressed, and referred to, in the same way as Suzuki-san the derivatives salesman. The suffix 'san' is the Japanese equivalent of 'Mr/Mrs/Miss', except it never changes, neither according to sex nor marital status. If I was not careful, massive over-compensation (or under-compensation) could occur.

At one stage we needed new office space, and the collapse of a famous US hedge fund finally gave us the chance to get our hands on some, but we were held up by the fact that neither my own staff nor the landlord would sign the lease until an auspicious day in the Buddhist calendar. I sometimes found it hard to remember that Japan was in the G7.

My familiarity with tatami (woven reed matting) increased as the negotiations for additional space continued. The new space was not covered with tatami and we were not propos-ing to install it, but I had to learn very quickly how many tatami mats would fit into it. This is because the principal unit of measurement in Japan is the *tsubo*. One *tsubo* is equiv-alent to two tatami mats. Clear? I finally managed to get someone to explain to me that a tatami mat measured 1.8m by 0.9m. This is not a joke – commercial rents in Japan are quoted in yen per *tsubo* per month. When I did my MBA they never told me that one of my toughest management tasks would be to estimate how many tatami mats made up one dealing desk.

* * *

I learned to survive disasters. One day the lights in the office all went out at 10.30 a.m. I was standing on the dealing floor, talking to my boss, when they flickered and then failed altogether. In the few seconds that it took for the back-up generator to spring into action, my corporate life flashed before my eyes; where exactly *was* the contingency plan? Had the computer line to the Tokyo Stock Exchange gone down? Were we in the middle of a trade? Was it an earthquake? I still hadn't ordered the fireproof filing cabinet for the HR records! Fortunately we were in an office block well-prepared for such eventualities and so were without power for less than ten seconds. Other properties that received power from the same source as us were not so lucky. The electricity generating company was prepared for an earthquake, but not for a Japanese military jet crashing into its main power lines. Some households were apparently without power for more than twenty-four hours. There was the statutory press conference at which the managers bowed deeply to express their apologies for the incident.

A disaster plan is more necessary for survival in Tokyo than in most financial centres. There are about one thousand earthquakes a year in Japan, most of which can be detected only by specialist seismic monitoring equipment. Most of them occur in the Kanto region, in which Tokyo is situated. Tokyo itself has not had a major earthquake since 1923, when it was struck by one that measured about seven on the

Richter scale. This destroyed about a third of the city. On average, Tokyo has had a major earthquake every sixty years or so, so it is well overdue for one now.

Disaster planning is necessary at the personal as well as the professional level. I confess that in all my time there I did nothing apart from ensure that we had the requisite water supplies at home (three litres per person per day) and some spare batteries for the torch. I remember looking in the larder and thinking that, if we survived, we would be living on baby-milk formula, salsa and tinned spaghetti. Oh, and tomato ketchup.

Somehow I seem to have missed all the earthquakes that occurred while I lived in Japan, but maybe it's not that easy to tell. My Single Girlfriend tells me that her first earthquake experience in Japan took place at 3 a.m., and she did not realise what was going on at all. She awoke to find the bed shaking. She turned over and addressed her then boyfriend in the dark. 'Hugh,' she apparently said, 'are you having a wank?'

Japan was wonderful and I loved every minute. In contrast, being a working expatriate mother in Hong Kong was not an especially happy experience. When I was preparing to leave England for Hong Kong, people were congratulating me on the move and pointing out how much cheaper childcare was there. A Filipina amah was to be had for a fraction of the price of a UK nanny. But of course there are two major draw-backs to this, which make Hong Kong a particularly difficult posting for any working mother. The first is that Filipina amahs, while certainly costing a fraction of what a trained nanny does, are also capable of a fraction of what a trained nanny can do. The housework and babysitting are fine, but organising developmental activities around the kitchen table in the afternoons, arranging play dates with other children, supervising homework and, in particular, keeping household discipline are all beyond the capabilities of any Filipina amah in Hong Kong. In the end I survived by doing what I should have done in the first place and hiring an English nanny as well. This exercise was considerably hampered by the size of staff accommodation in Hong Kong, in which en suite facilities consist of a shower running onto a tiled area of floor and a lavatory in the corner of the room. So I was obliged to find a living-out nanny who was paying exorbitant Hong Kong rent somewhere else and had to be compensated accordingly.

The second reason why Hong Kong is such a terrible place for working expatriate mothers is that the school day is short and non-school activities centre around expatriate clubs. But if little Johnny wants to go swimming, do art or play cricket with his peers in the excellent classes run by such august establishments as the Hong Kong Cricket Club or the Hong Kong Country Club, his parents have to be members and he has to be taken there and back in the afternoons. So far so good. While almost no Filipina amah can drive, there are plentiful and cheap taxis. However, with one notable exception, no expatriate club in Hong Kong will allow domestic servants inside their establishments, so if you work Johnny can't go to swimming club if he is too small to be just dropped off and picked up an hour and a half later. The club will certainly not take responsibility for changing little Johnny and then drying him and putting him back into his clothes afterwards. The mother – not the amah – is expected to do this, and the mother is also expected to be at the poolside the whole time to admire and applaud his efforts in the water.

Of course, virtually no expatriate mothers work, and the Chinese mothers who work don't face the same issues because their children are doing activities in places where domestic servants are allowed, and they have their families to support and look after the children. Their children are also allowed to stay up incredibly late at night and end up having naps in the afternoon, which is one way of keeping them occupied until you get home from work. My mother was thousands of miles away, and I can't abide children anywhere near me after 7.30 at night, so I was not going to be able to follow the Chinese pattern.

Mr M was also working in Hong Kong and travelling around Asia, and we tried hard to make sure that we were never both out of the country at the same time. In August 1994, when I was almost seven months pregnant with son number two, I was asked to go as part of a due diligence team to visit a company in Madras, India, at a time when Mr M was in Taiwan. Due diligence is not an exciting exercise. Prior to the issue of any new shares in a company, or before it is sold to another one, its business and financial statements will be examined in great detail by a team of people from the sponsoring bank, and usually outside lawyers and accountants as well.

Not wishing to leave son number one to the ministrations of a Filipina amah of dubious quality, and not having yet bitten the bullet and hired an English nanny, I saw no alternative but to take him with me. I flew into Madras and checked into the Sheraton Towers, explaining to the extremely helpful staff there that I had arrived to do a three-day project with my four-year-old child in tow. The hotel staff were fantastic and looked after son number one while I worked in a spartan office on the other side of Madras.

The due diligence team included our corporate finance team from Bombay and a lawyer from Allen & Overy, who had flown over from the UK. The lawyer was exceptionally well educated on the subject of Indian temples, and spent every spare minute visiting them. In the evening I would rejoin my son, who always seemed to have had a spectacular day riding on elephants or swimming in the hotel pool.

Our task completed, the day I was due to leave (to make a presentation the next morning to Malaysia Telecom on the bank's capabilities in convertible bonds), feeling uncomfortable and hot, I changed into more comfortable Indian clothing for the coming journey. This was the shalwar-kameez (drawstring trousers and a very long top), which did not hide my advanced pregnancy but at least covered it up without being too restricting. Standing at the hotel reception desk paying my bill in fancy dress, my four-year-old over-excitedly running up and down the corridor shrieking at the top of his voice, I thought it was just as well that we were a long way from any of the bank's offices.

Unbeknown to me, the bank had sent somebody from head office in Europe to inspect the IT systems in Bombay and had suggested that he might like to drop in on the due diligence team in Madras to see an example of the bank in action. He walked into the hotel as I was paying the bill and asked the manager where the senior bank personnel were. The manager indicated the pregnant lady in Indian clothing paying the bill, complete with four-year-old shrieking son tearing up and down the corridors. Rather taken aback, he approached me and asked me whether I really was bank personnel. I assured him that I was, and indeed had spent three days slaving away here. 'And where are the rest of your team?' he asked. I could truthfully tell him that our corporate finance team and the client were in the local discotheque, and the man from Allen & Overy was in bed reading a very large book on Indian temples. I, on the other hand, resplendent in national dress, was about to take a flight to Kuala Lumpur. He looked even more horrified. 'But you are pregnant and with a small child.' I will not repeat what my reaction to this was, but suffice to say that he retired to bed and the next morning booked himself on the first flight out, pleading a severe case of 'Delhi belly'.

* * *

Originally I went to Hong Kong to be the head of investment research for Asia. This was a bit of a joke, as there were not really very many people to be head of, but I did manage to scrape together a team, and between us we covered everything from cement factories in Pakistan to tobacco companies in Australia. We were also supporting the corporate finance department, whose sole aim was to be appointed adviser for companies doing deals. I spent the whole of 1994 flying from country to country making presentations with corporate finance on company valuations to prove how incredibly knowledgeable we as a bank were on every subject under the sun. Underwater telephone cables, wind-generated electricity, cash-and-carry supermarkets – you name it, I became an instant expert on it.

After a year of this I metamorphosed into a corporate finance person myself, which I hated – it lasted six months. Corporate finance origination, i.e. *winning* business (as opposed to execution, which means *doing* deals), takes sycophancy to heights never before seen by man. The purpose is to win corporate business for the bank, as I mentioned, but it is boringly narrow – it really means winning deals specifi-cally in the share market, and occasionally the debt security market. I was much more interested in the whole relation-ship a global bank can have with its corporate clients: starting with their particular needs (they need to build a television factory in China, they want to buy a supermarket chain in Thailand, they wish to explore for oil off the coast of Indone-sia or buy three new aeroplanes) and then seeing what financing route looks best.

So I moved on to an area of banking called structured finance, where the range of banking products you can offer to your client is far wider than just issuing new shares for them. I loved building and managing relationships with corporate clients in Asia and was soon happily settled. One evening my old boss, the global head of investment research, was passing through Hong Kong with a chap who had newly arrived at the bank to run global equity sales. Would I have dinner with them at the Mandarin Grill?

The dinner was wonderful, and I was even presented with a Hermès scarf, for some reason that has long since escaped me. (Even after fifteen years of collecting and some twenty-five scarves later, I am always ecstatic when some-one has shelled out £170 and bought me a Hermès scarf. Let's face it, a girl can't have too many. For my thirty-third birthday I hired a ski chalet in Canada and invited eight friends to stay from the UK. On the day of my birthday three of them, including my Most Glamorous Girlfriend and my Most Successful Girlfriend, produced Hermès scarves for me – they looked crestfallen as they realised they had been unoriginal, but I was on cloud nine. And none of them was the same!) The three of us had some excellent food and wine and chatted about the importance of client relationship management. Tanked up with champagne, I expanded on my theories of proper client service. The new boy had to leave and catch the midnight flight back to the UK. My former boss and I then got stuck into the port and were reminiscing about the good old days when the waiter came across. There was a telephone call for me, he said. Could I come over to the cashier's desk and take it?

Rather puzzled by this, I got up and went over to the desk. Surely it couldn't be Mr M, calling to check up on me? It was still only 10.30, and he knew I was with two men who had both long settled down with their respective partners, and neither of whom was going to carry me off (or even lead me off – I'm a bit heavy to carry) to their bedroom suite.

In fact it was the chap who had just left for the airport. He apologised for disrupting the final stages of the dinner and then said he had been giving my views on clients some thought (by my calculations, all of twenty minutes' worth). They sounded exactly what the bank should be doing to manage their relationships with their fund management clients, not just their corporate clients. Would I move back to the UK – preferably next week – and work for him?

It was a year before the People's Republic of China were due to take over from the British, and a move back to the UK seemed an appealing idea. I wasn't worried about any potential loss of political freedom, but I knew that life would never be the same after the British military presence in Hong Kong pulled out and closed down its radio station. The British Forces Broadcasting Service has the highly sensible policy (not adopted by the World Service, I am sad to say) of including the omnibus edition of 'The Archers' in its weekly programming. In 1996 the BBC did not (as they do now) e-mail me a synopsis every day. A return to Radio 4 was a very exciting proposition. I accepted, and thus went to work for a man who had hired me on his way to the airport – my Far Too Nice Boss.

* * *

My ability to survive in the financial centres of the world was due partly to my readiness to try anything to succeed. Getting investment research published out of Hong Kong in 1994, when I didn't have access to any desktop publishing software or anyone to operate it, looked to be impossible. In those days before e-mail (hard to believe now) I simply tracked down the modem used to send the monthly accounts to head office and hijacked it to send text and figures instead, getting them formatted, printed and air-freighted back, using the bulk discounts with the freight company that our head office enjoyed and the distribution lists they already had in place. My strategy – namely, to assume that there was always a solution to every problem, you just had to find it – invariably worked. It helped, of course, that regulations are different everywhere; no restrictions on entertaining fund managers are in evidence in Japan or Hong Kong, that's for sure.

The other factor that stood me in good stead throughout all three overseas postings was my internal network within the bank. The colleagues I befriended in the first two years, and the two years I spent in London between Hong Kong and Singapore, helped me meet the many challenges I faced overseas. These people included directors of the bank's main board, and many senior managers, but more importantly they included the switchboard operator in London, the catering manager at head office, the human resources department, and the publications manager in Europe. To this day I look back on my nine years in the City and think gratefully of the support these people provided. My advice to people wanting to survive in any jungle, but especially the City, is to treat everyone with respect and show an interest in them. Everyone will have something to contribute one day. If that doesn't appeal to your survival instincts, try this: be careful whose heads you clamber over on your way to the top, as they will be attached to the backsides you will have to kiss on the way down.

Returning to London in the spring of 1996 was challenging, too. I had two children aged eighteen months and six, and Mr M was not coming. We had not separated, were not getting divorced; on the contrary, we had just decided to try for a third baby, and I had even gone to the time and trouble of having my coil removed. But his contract with the vast media empire had not expired and he was required to stay. I moved him into a one-bedroom serviced apartment, made arrangements for a twice-weekly cleaner, bought him a new microwave and then got on the plane home. For the next two years I lived as a single parent in London, flying to see my husband every four or eight weeks (and as my fertility cycle is more like twenty-six days than twenty-eight, this was a carefully calculated exercise). After a couple of false starts, I did manage to conceive son number three, but only after we had finally been reunited in Singapore. Thus I arrived in Japan heavily pregnant. Two years later, I was offered another chance to return to the UK, and this time Mr M was able to commit to following me within months rather than years. I breathed a sigh of relief. I had done my time overseas, had survived, and was coming home, this time for good.

Chapter 9

Leaving the City

Leaving the City

N THE SPRING OF 2000 I was brought back from Japan to be the number two to a wonderful man whom I adored. A former Bank of England economist, he was well read, well spoken and great company, and was someone I could learn a lot from. It was he who had taken me to dinner in the Mandarin Grill, who had presented me with the exquisite Hermès scarf, who had visited me in Japan, in Australia, in Singapore. I would have walked over burning coals for this man, and I happily relocated children, nanny and housekeeper from Tokyo to London.

My new and much-adored boss had not long since had a major heart operation, and the purpose of my return was to relieve him of some of his workload. I arrived in the office bright and early on a Monday to take up my new duties. 'I have news for you, Mrs M,' he said. 'I have decided to give up work altogether and retire.'

This was the beginning of the end as far as I was concerned. The City is not about money, it is about people. I tried to console myself by entering into discussions with another of my favourite people, the man who had persuaded me all those years ago to return for another interview after the debacle with the smaller-companies salesman. Nine years later he was considerably more senior, the glasses had been replaced by contact lenses, the buttons on the shirts had given way to cufflinks and the shirts themselves were of a superior fabric so that you could no longer glimpse the vest underneath. However, although he welcomed the idea of my working for him, I was persuaded by our overall boss, the man who had sent me to Japan, that I should remain where I was for the time being until the replacement for the departing cardiac patient had arrived and settled in.

What a mistake that was. For a start, she arrived and persuaded the bank to also hire her people, who were installed immediately. On the day of her arrival I got up extra early so that I could personally go over her office with a duster and can of Pledge, a reminder that however senior and well paid you are in the City there are still menial tasks to be performed.

Being nursemaid to someone is not a satisfying career, and no matter what I did to support her I never got any thanks. Navigating through the bank's paperwork to set her up as a signatory for expenses, arranging to hire her support team from her previous bank, ensuring that she was introduced to the people that mattered – none of this was appreciated. The other problem was simply that, while investment banking and stockbroking can be great fun when you are involved in them yourself, managing other people who are involved is not. Management in investment banking, as anywhere, is about resolving disputes, allocating resources, cutting costs and making difficult hiring and firing decisions. It is not about the two things I had always enjoyed in the City – spending time with both fund managers and corporate clients.

Then the bank made a number of appointments to the main board, including someone for whom I had much professional respect but had never liked – and he had never liked me. Fortunately I was still too junior for it to matter much, although the next step up would have brought me into direct conflict with him. It was definitely time to exit, especially as the man I had selected as my next boss, he of the superior shirts, now had no vacancies, despite having previously said otherwise.

* * *

I probably left the City just in time. While I have been writing this book I have continually read or heard of enforced departures as investment banks clear the decks and prepare to batten down the hatches for what they expect to be a long and painful crawl back to 'normal' market volumes. I left at the end of October 2000. A month later, the revenue streams started to dry up, although I cannot flatter myself that the two events are connected. I was of course making a lifestyle choice rather than taking a view on world stock markets, but the truth is that part of that choice was very much to do with how the industry scales up – and down. No job is secure in the twenty-first century, but investment banking jobs are less secure than most. I had been around long enough to know that one's friends and colleagues could be here today and gone tomorrow, never to be mentioned again, and with their contributions forgotten instantly.

More than any other industry, investment banking is about being rewarded for future prospects rather than past performance. Bonus time is the ultimate example of this. You may have won and executed the merger of the two biggest companies in the world last year, but the bonus you get (unless you are clever enough to have negotiated a guarantee) will depend upon what revenue you are likely to write over the coming year. Many of my former colleagues located outside Europe had their 2000 bonuses almost completely deferred from March to July, and then made conditional on achieving first-half 2001 targets. So much for the theory that this bonus was supposed to reflect performance in 2000.

Never expect thanks, either. In nine years, no one in the bank ever said thank you to me for any work I did that generated income (or cut costs) for our shareholders. They said thank you for other things: writing speeches, organising parties, collecting dry cleaning, booking honeymoon hotels, and so on. But never for doing my job.

Of course, investment bankers earn so much more than the average citizen that clearly a risk premium is being paid, and so it could be argued that job losses are an acceptable occupational hazard. But remember, this is, more than any other, an industry built on relationships. There are always going to be consequences for chucking people onto the slag heap.

In 2001, one of the Arrogant Twosome became such a casualty. The duo had parted company many years before, when the younger reinvented himself and subsequently pushed off to a heavyweight US investment bank. Now the elder of the two had to part company, unwillingly, with the bank we had both worked for. Fifteen years of service were dispensed with by less than ten minutes of prepared speech from his manager and the delegated HR official. Security pass confiscated, he was allowed back to his desk briefly to collect his possessions before driving himself home in time for morning coffee. The team that he had left behind told me that, to them, it felt like a bereavement. Oxbridge-educated, with an excellent brain, he was anything but complacent about his job. He had two outstanding qualities which, if I were a shareholder in the bank, I would have been sad to lose. He was wise enough to understand the commercial needs of a modern investment bank and ensure that his actions benefited as many departments as possible. Also, in an unobtrusive way, he was the most remarkable nurturer of young talent. His team members have without exception gone on to great success, myself being the least of these. One provides critical support for a very high-profile female fund manager, another is one of the most highly rated analysts in the world, working for the Yanks in Canary Wharf. And there are many more. Learning to be a good investment analyst, with all the skills that takes – not just number-crunching, but marketing (internally and externally), dealing with corporate clients, understanding the industry drivers – is what I and many others had learned from him.

Of course, recessions are a good time for a clear-out, and in banks as anywhere else there are always people who are just passengers and deserve to be kicked off the train, but are such wholesale sackings necessary? And are the consequences really thought through? If I had any lingering regrets about leaving the City, they disappeared the week my colleague was shown the door.

Five months later, the bank wiped out two further years of my working life with another sweep of the red pen. One hundred and twenty people were made redundant. Events like this happen regularly, but this time, as they say in the films, it was personal. Almost without exception, the entire batch had worked for me while I was in Japan. The business I had nurtured, fought for, steered through choppy waters (including two regulatory inspections and the deregulation of commissions) was removed from the map. A few people are still there, and the bank claims that it remains committed to Japan (I believe it – how can you be global without being in Japan?) but as far as I am concerned the guts of the business, effectively my family for a while, had been ripped out.

Of course, the Nikkei was at a seventeen-year low and Japan was suffering a horrible recession, not helped by the fact that even a reforming prime minister was finding it difficult to drive legislation through. The really extraordinary thing, though, is how I came to hear about the proposed wholesale sackings, the day before the actual event. The Japanese office ran a central diary for people to see what clients were being marketed to by whom. For some reason (deliberate?) the management inserted into this scheduler appointments with outplacement agencies and even set aside time for handling press enquiries. Needless to say this did not pass unnoticed by the members of staff who happened to log on. At least it gave everyone psychological preparation time, but then this is like knowing that someone has a terminal illness – you know they are going to die, but it is no less upsetting when it happens.

I am sure that many of you will have little sympathy with job losses in the Square Mile. There is a school of thought that says, 'Why shed tears over the demise of another few bankers? They're all rich and over-paid anyway,' and I understand this view. Many of those who are losing their jobs now have been over-paid for years, and if they have been prudent with their money they will not be facing severe hardship. The salaries and bonuses enjoyed by many investment bankers are high precisely because there is no job security; and many of them conveniently forget this. My sadness over the decision to cut the Japanese business was more to do with my own sweat and tears, for which I was not uncommonly well paid (remember, I'm a woman), and also with the manner in which my former colleagues were dismissed. (In Japan culture dictates that – unless you are being dismissed for disciplinary reasons – you should at least be allowed to e-mail all your contacts and clients to alert them of your departure; this was effectively denied my former colleagues. They were assembled in a hotel function room to be told of their fate, and when they returned to their desks to collect their possessions they found that their computer access and telephone lines had been cut.)

In many cases botched decisions are the inevitable result of putting people in positions of authority who have no appropriate management skills, simply because they are good at their existing job. It does not follow that if someone is good at structuring complex financial transactions they will be good at managing people. As a manager who has made these difficult decisions myself, I know it isn't easy. If you have two people up for promotion, one with better finance skills than the other, who has better management skills, you are still almost always going to promote the former because he or she will command the respect of their peers.

* * *

What do people do when they leave the City? Many of them start businesses. The founder of New Covent Garden Soups, Andrew Palmer, was once in the City. So was Luke Johnson, CEO of Belgo. The proprietor of the *Financial News*, Angus

Macdonald, had a brief career in investment management when he was much younger. When you have stood on the sidelines advising or selling, being a small cog in a big wheel, there is nothing more satisfying that being able to own your own company and dictate your own agenda. Others join non-City businesses, becoming finance directors or in-house corporate financiers. Again, these people tell me how good it is to be on the inside rather than advisers on the outside.

There are also many who represent the triumph of hope over experience and leave big broking forms to start small ones. Sometimes these succeed, other times they fail. One of my girlfriends, the granddaughter of one of Britain's most famous architects, joined a famous City investment bank straight after her graduation from Oxford, specialising in Japanese stocks and shares. From that day until she was arbitrarily laid off with her colleagues she followed the Japanese market daily and spent hours studying its up and downs (most recently downs, as we know). She was considered an excellent stockbroker by her fund management clients, who happily followed her as she moved to three other banks during her career. When her career as a stockbroker ended involuntarily in the autumn of 2001, she started a hedge fund with a few former colleagues. This required her to take some quite advanced examinations in order to achieve acceptable status with the regulatory authorities. She passed them after much hard work, and devoted a great deal of effort and energy to trying to get her hedge fund off the ground. But no one wanted to be the first investor. They all promised her funds as and when she could find the first person to write a cheque. I have always said that fund managers are sometimes able to make sheep look like mature and independent thinkers. She finally gave up and moved to France.

What of my other girlfriends? I never persuaded my Most Glamorous Girlfriend to leave advertising for the City, but I managed the next best thing – I introduced her to someone else I worked with at the bank, and she is now happily married with a beautiful son, my godson, and has become the model City wife. My Most Socially Acceptable Girlfriend broke free from the Arrogant Twosome as I left for Hong Kong and initially went to work for another leading investment analyst in a different bank. He proved to be an inspirational boss, and he had been married so many times that there was no danger of him retiring. However, after a few years she retired from the City temporarily to do an MBA, and when she returned did so as a fund manager, swapping from the sell side to the buy side. Now she is fawned over by male stockbrokers and analysts, rather than doing the fawning herself, and is no doubt subjected regularly to the chocolate knickers treatment.

When I left the City the children were mightily relieved to hear that I was not about to become a full-time mother. I did, however, want to watch the occasional rugby match on a Wednesday afternoon and not just call in from Kuala Lumpur for the result, to attend carol services, to read with my six-year-old and check his spelling, and even to hug and kiss the baby (despite the fact that he thought the nanny was his mother). I also still wanted to work, to be part of an office, to interact daily with people who have a common purpose and a shared philosophy, to engage in debate, to follow and be part of current affairs. I am happier doing that than changing nappies – as Mr M often points out, my nappy-changing technique is useless. But this time I was determined to be part of the decision-making process in the company I joined, which meant buying a big chunk of the shares.

Abandoning the sheltered and privileged world of a glass-fronted, air-conditioned office in EC2, I started work in a room shared by three others where the only ventilation is a window. This, when opened, ensures that anything on my desk immediately relocates to the floor. Do I regret it? No. Am I richer? In monetary terms, most definitely not. In lifestyle terms, most definitely yes.

Working in a small company was always going to be a culture shock after being part of an organisation that employed nearly 100,000 people in more than seventy countries. I had to learn quickly that it is not possible to change the way a company is run overnight, especially if it has been going for twenty years before you even showed up. On arrival I discovered there to be no dishwasher, and had to wage a long campaign to buy one. In the end, I took a unilateral decision to purchase one on my company credit card and had it delivered while my partners were on holiday. Only then did I discover the extent of the replumbing that had to be undertaken to accommodate it, which cost twice as much as the appliance itself.

The economic slowdown (we are still not technically in recession) has certainly affected our company. However, I feel it is possible that here my own efforts will directly affect our performance, whereas my sweat and tears as one of the 100,000 employees of my previous employer were as drops in the ocean. No wonder I swapped a global banking operation for a tiny little company in W1.

I miss many things about the City, not least the annual bonus cheque, although presumably it would be a tad smaller if not non-existent by now. I miss the exceptionally generous defined pension scheme of which I was a non-contributory member, although this is now closed to new joiners. I miss many of the people, although I still see several of them, and in any case the real characters in the City are rapidly being replaced by hordes of identikit Oxbridge graduates.

I do not miss the 7 a.m. starts, the endless travelling, the greed and the egos, the annual grind of budgeting and bonuses. I certainly do not miss working round the clock for a lot of faceless shareholders.

I look back on my time in the City with much affection, but have never regretted my decision to leave. I joined the bank on the threshold of my thirties, an impoverished cricket widow living in a damp Pimlico basement. I left it more than eight years later, a less impoverished golf widow living in London and Oxfordshire. Eight years had seen me through five country moves and ten kilograms of weight gain, and although the nightmare of not being able to pay the school fees had receded, I was more than ready to step off the tread-mill.

I survived. I both joined and left the City at a time of my own choosing, in hindsight a remarkable feat. I made some enemies, but I made many more friends. I learned that I am unusually fascinated by how the machinations of the City feed the financial needs of growing companies. But in the end, if I was to continue surviving, I needed to get off that particular roundabout and climb aboard another.

Afterword

More than two years after I left the City, I look back and wonder how I ever survived at all. I was too old (30) when I went in, too clever for some jobs and not clever enough for others, not ambitious enough, too strident a personality to be easily accepted. Above all, I was a girl, and the odds were stacked against me, as I have said – not because the City is sexist (although it is) but because being a wife and mother does not sit easily alongside a career that requires you to be at someone else's beck and call twenty-four hours a day.

I got my job in the City during what I realise now was an economic slowdown (as opposed to a recession, which, as you will recall me pointing out to the cabbie, is a technical term requiring two successive quarters of negative economic growth). That alone demonstrated my ability to survive, and shows that tenacity is a trait worth equipping oneself with when scaling the City's walls. I then set to in order to catch up for lost time and learn a trade and a whole way of life completely from scratch, regardless of how many weekends I had to spend filing company documents or reading five-year-old annual reports to work out when some division or other had been acquired or disposed of. The important thing in the City is never to stop learning – the day it has nothing new to teach you is the day you should quit.

I am not the cleverest person on the planet, despite a string of academic achievements. I was clever enough, though, to work out that many of the people I sat among on the trading floor were lazy or bored, or so convinced of their own self-worth that they had long forgotten what we were all in business to do – to make our fund management clients more money by helping them achieve better investment performance. To some extent this is simply a question of helping them do their job – e-mailing them financial models, giving them company data they can't access, or setting up meetings with CEOs they haven't got the time or energy to contact but would like to meet. All these things will make their life easier, and therefore make it more likely that they will succeed in achieving their professional goals, and consequently reward you.

Have you ever been to a restaurant or hotel where the service was exemplary? Where every time you picked up the telephone to room service or the front desk they answered immediately and fulfilled your every request? That is how I believe a stockbroker should deal with a fund manager. The City is a service business. The basis of a service business is that clients need to be serviced. Remembering this simple principle is perhaps the most vital survival tip.

* * *

Five years from now, will the City be full of independent research firms and, under separate ownership, corporate finance advice companies? I doubt it. I appreciate the merits of independent investment research, and so do fund management companies, but they are not going to pay for it. Like corporate social responsibility, independent research is admirable, but at the end of the day unlikely to catch on unless legislation requires it. Until there is a definitive study showing that corporate social responsibility directly increases return on capital employed, I doubt that the majority of public companies will do more than pay lip service to it. Equally, until genuine value-added independent investment research can be produced at a quarter of the price it costs right now, it will always have to be subsidised by the advice brokers give to public companies, whether directly or indirectly.

I have a true survival story to illustrate this. A man I have known for fifteen years, a qualified medical doctor, used to be a real-life Andrew Analyst, working as a highly rated pharmaceutical analyst for a leading London investment bank. His recommendations moved share prices, but his salary and bonus were undoubtedly subsidised by the profits his employer made from advising public companies, including pharmaceutical ones.

But he quit. After going back to university for a year (like me, to the London Business School), he changed his life completely. He swapped the Saab for a bicycle, bachelorhood for marriage and fatherhood, and highly paid employment for a more precarious financial existence running his own company. What did it do? It provided independent research on pharmaceutical companies. Other than recommending whether or not to buy or sell the shares, it would tell you everything you wanted to know about Novartis or GlaxoSmithKline, or even smaller biotech companies, all superbly modelled on powerful computers and with genuine value-added commentary.

Was it an overnight success? No. I am pleased to report that it is very successful now, but it was very slow to get started and even today its primary customers are the pharmaceutical companies themselves, keen to learn about their competitors. If Eliot Spitzer is right, my friend's company has a very bright future – provided that fund managers realise its worth.

* * *

Do I think the City will continue to be male dominated and a challenging environment for women to work in? Yes and yes, but these are not necessarily bad things. It will continue to be male dominated, as so many other industries are, because (a) women are less inclined than men to work in the financial services sector and (b) women are more inclined than men to take on the majority of home-making tasks. It will therefore still be challenging, not intellectually but because the long hours and the nature of the business as a service industry will continue to pose a challenge to any woman.

Surviving as a woman in the City is not that hard. With all those male egos in such a confined space, there couldn't be a better place to be a woman! You don't have to look like Julia Roberts or even Melinda Messenger to get your own way. I, for example, am seriously nothing to look at. I recently heard that one of the more senior men I worked with for many years in the City told a newspaper editor that during all that time he could never work out whether I was pregnant or not. (I shall take a charitable view of this and assume it was because I never bothered to take any maternity leave.) Equally, there is another senior member of staff who has never to this day addressed me by name – to my face he just grunts and behind my back I am referred to as 'Thunderthighs'.

Yet even for me the chocolate knickers treatment invariably worked. Any female investment banker who is able to sit in rapt attention (verging on adoration) as the male finance director of a public company describes his amortisation policy will ultimately find that he enjoys doing business with her. Similarly, treating every male fund manager as though they were Tom Cruise, Richard Gere and Brad Pitt rolled into one will usually ensure a certain amount of business, even if you have given them terrible investment advice.

Is this selling your soul? I don't think so. As I said earlier, if it is legal and it makes money, then fine. I don't think of myself as equal to men. In many respects, I think of women as more capable than men – they are better at multi-tasking, much less linear in their thinking. Mr M, for example, is capable of getting himself ready to go and play golf, or making breakfast for the children, or dealing with the laundry. But all three simultaneously? Forget it.

Ultimately survival in the City is like survival anywhere else. You have to really want to be there, and be prepared to work hard to survive. Yes, it is an industry that can easily accommodate a variety of intellectual capabilities, but however clever or otherwise you are, the one thing you cannot be is lazy. Work hard, be effective, and you will survive.

Recommended Reading

Bryan Burrough, John Helyar, *Barbarians at the Gate: The Fall of RJR Nabisco*, HarperPerennial, 1993

Recounts the $25 billion battle for control of RJR Nabisco, reputedly the largest takeover in Wall Street history. I read this book when it first came out, couldn't put it down, and stayed up into the small hours devouring it. It remains one of the best books about a deal ever written, and will teach you what a leveraged buyout and a contested bid really are, along with lessons about how a company's management are sometimes their own worst enemies. Great also at describing the relationship between companies and their advisers.

Michael Lewis, *Liar's Poker: Two Cities, True Greed*, Coronet, 1999

This is the book I wish I had written: entertaining, readable, an insider's view of what it is like to work on the legendary Salomon bond-dealing floor. Introduces readers to a cast of (real) characters, many of who reappear in *When Genius Failed* (see below).

James B. Stewart, *Den of Thieves*, Simon & Schuster, 1992

An account of how Ivan Boesky, Michael Milken and their accomplices created a series of financial frauds on a vast scale, and of the chase that finally brought them to justice. The author is a Pulitzer Prize-winning journalist who also wrote *The Partners* and *The Prosecutors*. This is the book that will tell you what junk bonds are (see p. 26) and describes the Wall Street that the film character Gordon Gekko, he of the 'greed is good' speech, inhabited. There are other books about Drexel Burnham Lambert but this was the one I liked most.

John Gapper and Nicholas Denton, *All That Glitters: The Fall of Barings*, Hamish Hamilton, 1996

This is by far the best of the three books written on the Nick Leeson affair which brought down Barings Bank. I don't just say that because it was co-written by an *FT* colleague, John Gapper, but because it is well researched and written, and explains the story with minimal jargon and fascinating characterisations. I am not going to get precious about the misquoted Shakespeare of the title, despite the fact that *The Merchant of Venice* is my favourite play. (The first reader to write and tell me what the title should have been can have a free copy of this book signed by John Gapper.)

Lawrence Cunningham, *The Essays of Warren Buffett: Lessons for Investors and Managers*, revised ed., Wiley Eastern, 2002

If you read one book about investing in the stock market, make it this one. It is a compilation and extension of Warren

Buffett's letters to the shareholders in the company that he runs (see below). You could of course save your money and go to the Internet link I have given below, but there is much valuable commentary here that will enable you to place Buffett's comments in context.

Frank Partnoy, *F.I.A.S.C.O.: Guns, Booze and Bloodlust: The Truth about High Finance*, Profile, 1998

Now we are getting to slightly more challenging territory. Frank Partnoy describes very complicated financial products in as straightforward a way as possible, while providing plenty of real-life examples of biased, arrogant and overconfident behaviour on Wall Street. Here you will find out what asset-backed securities and fixed income derivatives (see p. 26) are. As one reviewer said, if you still believe in market efficiency and investor rationality, this book is 'a great reality check'. It's not *Liar's Poker*, but a worthwhile book nonetheless.

Roger Lowenstein, *When Genius Failed: The Rise and Fall of Long Term Capital Management*, Fourth Estate, 2002

If the preceding books are easy for beginners, here is a slightly more difficult one which explains how John Meriweather, hot from the pages of *Liar's Poker* (see above), made and lost a fortune the size of which most of us can only try to imagine. He's still out there trying again! It's enjoyable and informative, but don't make it the first book on the list that you read or you might miss the finer points.

Recommended Reading

Tony Golding, *The City: Inside the Great Expectation Machine: Myth and Reality in Institutional Investment and the Stock Market*, Financial Times/Prentice-Hall, 2002

This is really the companion volume to *Survival in the City*, in that it also explains the broker/fund manager relationship in a readable but far more detailed manner than my own offering. Here's a puzzle for you: I write another column under a different pseudonym, which appears on the Internet. Tony Golding thought that my fictitious character was real and quotes her in his book. What is her name? (Clue: she appears after p. 200.)

Philip Augar, *The Death of Gentlemanly Capitalism: The Rise and Fall of London's Investment Banks*, Penguin, 2001

Philip Augar has a PhD in history from Cambridge and this is a meticulously researched history of the City, looking at how it came to be dominated by foreign-owned institutions over the last twenty years. It's not long on gossip or controversial opinion, and the funniest story is quoted by me in Chapter 1 above, but if you are planning to apply for a job in the City then it is a must-read prior to interview.

Romesh Vaitilingam, *The 'Financial Times' Guide to Using the Financial Pages*, Financial Times/Prentice-Hall, 2001

This tome from my alma mater, the *FT*, is the book I recommend to people who don't know how to mine the pink pages for relevant information. Another must for anyone considering a career in the City.

David Kynaston, *The City of London: A World of Its Own 1815–1890*, Pimlico, 1995
David Kynaston, *The City of London: 1914–1945*, Pimlico, 2000
David Kynaston, Will Sulkin (ed.), *The City of London: A Club No More, 1945–2000*, Pimlico, 2002

These three books comprise the most comprehensive history of the City and how it got to where it is today. If you enjoyed Philip Augar (see above), you will love these. For those of you with not much time, just read the final volume, which is also the heaviest!

Internet

www.berkshirehathaway.com/annual.html

This is where to find the real commentary on stock markets, how they work and what is wrong with them. It is contained each year in the annual letter to shareholders written by Warren Buffett, the CEO of Berkshire Hathaway, a US company that is essentially a holding company for the investments that Buffett and his team choose to make. Even in these times of depressed market prices, one 'A' share in Berkshire Hathaway costs c. US$69,000, so as there are not many shareholders Mr Buffett kindly posts the entire annual report on the Web for us all to read!

www.efinancialcareers.com

Here is the best place to go to find out about jobs and careers in the City. It is packed with editorial describing different jobs, pay structure, employment issues, and of course lots of ads for jobs. I am a regular contributor – here is where you will find the answer to the question posed in my review of Tony Golding's book above.

Finally, the Alex cartoon strip that adorns these pages appears daily in the *Daily Telegraph* and has inspired me ever since it was first published. I feel enormously honoured that its illustrator, Charles Peattie, has drawn my own cartoon and am thrilled that an Alex cartoon starts each of my chapters. For those of you unfamiliar with Alex, his website address is www.alexcartoon.com, at which site you can find information on all the Alex books published.